THE PASTOR
as
SPIRITUAL
GUIDE

THE PASTOR
as
SPIRITUAL
GUIDE

Howard Rice

UPPER
ROOM BOOKS®
NASHVILLE

THE PASTOR AS SPIRITUAL GUIDE

Cover design: Gore Studio / www.gorestudio.com
Cover images: sky image, Corbis; compass image, Comstock
Third printing: 2004

Library of Congress Cataloging-in-Publication

Rice, Howard L.
    The pastor as spiritual guide / Howard Rice.
          p.   cm.
    Includes bibliographical references.
    ISBN 0-8358-0846-7
    1. Clergy—Office. 2. Pastoral theology. 3. Spiritual direction.
I. Title.
BV660.2.R53   1998   97-23359
253.5 ' 3—dc21   CIP

Printed in the United States of America on acid-free paper

Dedication

I DEDICATE THIS BOOK to all those pastors who have influenced my own ministry, who have been pastors and mentors throughout my life. They include my childhood pastor Arthur Oates, the pastor whose preaching became the voice of God in my call to ministry; Ray Kiely, my college preacher; G. Aubrey Young, whose preaching kept my faith alive during turbulent times; and the two preachers who kept me spiritually alive during seminary, Preston Bradley and Harrison Ray Anderson. During my first pastorate Jim Cayton and Roy Johnson, two mature pastors, took me under their wing and taught me more about being a pastor than I had learned in seminary. Kris Ronnow, who was then a college student, became my youth director; and Gladys Peek, a member of the congregation, became parish visitor. Together we formed a team in ministry. In my second pastorate, I remain deeply grateful for the colleagues in ministry who shared burdens and celebrated victories: Bob Davidson, Peggy Way, David Ramage, Jose Burgos, Priscilla Murray, and Henry Murray. In my years of seminary teaching, I once more became a church attender, sitting in the pew. My pastors have included John Najarian, Roy Scholobohm, Jean Richardson, Jeffrey Gaines, Wendy and Andrew Dreitcer; at present my pastors are Tom Nolen and Reford Nash.

All of these pastors have taught me, encouraged me, sustained and supported me, and helped me discover the real meaning of pastoral ministry. It is an honor to dedicate this book to them all and to express my gratitude even though some have gone on to claim the victory over death that is ours in Christ.

Contents

*Train yourself in godliness, for, while physical training is of
some value, godliness is valuable in every way,
holding promise for both the present life and the life to come.
The saying is sure and worthy of full acceptance.
For to this end we toil and struggle,
because we have our hope set on the living God,
who is the Savior of all people,
especially of those who believe.
—1 Timothy 4:7-10*

Pastoral Ministry as Vocation

THE PRACTICE OF THE ORDAINED MINISTRY today is in considerable turmoil and confusion. As a seminary professor and as a pastor, I have worked with and come to know hundreds of students who have become pastors. Sometimes I have had the painful experience of watching their heartbreak and anger at being caught up in the turmoil or damaged by the confusion. There is confusion about what a pastor does; there is confusion about how a pastor is to perform ministry. The number of books published each year on the subject of professional ministry, its theology and practice, is a clue to the confusion and attendant interest in the subject. Pastors buy these books, searching for a professional identity that has eluded them. In earlier decades pastors may have felt secure in the knowledge of who they were and what was expected of them; my own observation tells me this is no longer the case.

In our increasingly complex culture, the institutions that make up our society reflect that complexity. Every major institution is experiencing some change, and the professions connected to these institutions are not immune to that change.

The church has experienced several changes in its role and context. Churches, no longer the obvious molders and shapers of society, find their voice ignored or found laughable by the press. Many denominations, as a result of turmoil and conflict, find themselves caught in a polarization that tears at the fabric of the delicate unity holding them together. Whether the issue is civil rights, ordination of homosexuals, the role of the church in challenging unjust economic structures, or educational reform, never before—except in rare and painful situations—has the church endured such conflict. Today conflict seems part of the nature of being the church.

Many mainline congregations have experienced dramatic membership loss, which results in decline of income and a disheartening sense of failure. A majority of a generation has left organized religion, not choosing to return even when they began having children. Great numbers of young adults are absent from churches. Churches have suffered from displacement, conflict, and low self-esteem. Those who serve the church often find themselves caught in the cycle of blame that develops: *Someone must be at fault; surely there's a cause for our church's decline.* Pastors become scapegoats, easy targets for frustration and disappointment. Pastors may blame themselves for failure: "The church does not grow because I am not a good preacher." Or the professional staff may push themselves to try harder: "If I only worked more hours and made more calls, I might be able to change things."

Congregational demands and expectations have become more complex and varied. Some members expect the pastor to be a person of dignity who will bring prestige to the congregation by representing the church in the community. These members are unhappy that the present pastor does not have the prominence in the community that "dear old Doctor Jones" brought. Others want a pastor who is pleasant to be around and a good "mixer" with families and young people. When a pastor seeks time alone for study or prayer, they may view this behavior as a sign of haughtiness or lack of friendliness. Still others want a pastor who represents the depth our society lacks; they seek a pastor who asks challenging questions and inspires depth of thought in sermons. Today no pastor can please everyone or satisfy all expectations.

The large numbers of women entering the ordained ministry have generated further change in expectation. People do not quite know what to expect from women ministers. Many people still feel awkward in the presence of female clergy. Yet women pastors often are more open and receptive and more willing to relinquish long-held expectations than their male counterparts who may easily fall back upon traditional forms and seek to live out the expectations that have been around for a long time. With few role models, many women clergy work out their own ministerial approach and thus bring a more collegial style of working to pastoral ministry. The inclusion of women in previously male-dominated occupations has encouraged a leadership style of inclusion and cooperation rather than a style that operates from the top down. While some in society welcome this change, others miss the clear lines of authority.

At one time, the pastor was highly respected and treated with deference and dignity. That high status garnered some of the chief rewards of ministry, which meant that people valued the work of ministry. Men and women entered the ministry aware of the minimal financial rewards but also aware that parishioners and nonparishioners alike would accord them respect. They would have a clear and honored position in the community: their company sought out, their advice taken seriously, their words of wisdom treasured. Today fewer people take the position of pastor seriously. Parishioners no longer automatically accept the words of the pastor as worthy of serious contemplation.

In a largely secular society, the minister's useful functions are no longer obvious. The traditional duties of baptizing, officiating at weddings and funerals, and praying at public occasions have disappeared since many secular people have dispensed with these rituals altogether. Even among those persons searching for spiritual grounding, the church and its ministry may be the last place they look. They trust other gurus. They do not see that church pastors have much to say to them about the state of their souls.

Never has the practice of the ordained ministry been more difficult than at present. Many ministers show signs of wear, clues that they do not enjoy their work but find it a burden. They reveal signs of bitterness, anger, and unfulfilled expectations and dreams. I have heard a pastor say, "All the church members want is someone to hold their hands. They don't want a pastor who makes changes; that's why I'm quitting." As I visit congregations, it is not unusual to hear a parishioner complain, "The trouble with our pastor is that she doesn't visit like the others did. She's so busy with responsibilities outside the church that we hardly see her." Another former student complains, "The very gifts that I brought into the ministry are the last things I ever get to do; my people just aren't interested." Another parishioner confides, "Since my pastor came back from that church growth conference, all he wants to do is attract new people. We old-timers don't matter any more." Some pastors express their pain by directing anger toward the denomination; they become highly critical of programs and structures at the national or regional level. Other pastors direct their anger toward their spouses and families. The high clergy divorce rate indicates the difficulty of sustaining a healthy marriage while pastoring. Some clergy manifest their anger by making negative comments about parishioners, through surly attitudes, and in pastoral indifference. Something is seriously wrong with the practice of pastoral ministry when it produces such anger.

The contemporary situation may affect the more sensitive and caring pastors most deeply. They are the ones who leave the ministry or retire as early as possible in exhaustion in order to find space to put their lives back together. These pastors know they cannot fulfill all expectations without putting on the mask of hypocrisy. The unhappiness of many gifted pastors indicates role confusion and a lack of center for ministry.

This book's thesis is that the problems clergy face reveal the church's struggle with its own self-understanding. The church's lack of clarity about its mission results in lack of clarity related to the role of its clergy. Lack of clarity about expectations means that no matter what they do, pastors come under attack for not doing something quite different. More than any other issue, pastors complain that they spend their days doing what they never believed they would have to do so much. Many feel trapped in administrative work that is contrary to their sense of calling. The work to which they feel most called is often the activity least valued by parishioners. Pastors' concern with the sacred devolves into mundane business matters. Called and prepared to be soul makers and soul healers, pastors become CEOs. Church bureaucracy expects them to show a gain at the end of the year (of members and budget numbers) when they thought themselves called to be spokespersons for God. They spend days and nights in meetings wrangling over secular matters, when they believe themselves to have been sent to speak a word from the Lord to a particular people.

Clearly, part of what is wrong with pastoral ministry today is endemic to our culture. Every profession is hurting; its practitioners are feeling betrayed and abused. Doctors express their disillusionment by saying, "Medicine isn't fun any more." Lawyers tell self-deprecating jokes about themselves, and a majority of them indicate that if they had it to do over, they would take up some other line of work. School teachers complain about the problems of discipline, low parental support, and betrayal by the communities they seek to serve. Public servants feel demeaned.

When great numbers of people will not trust or respect anyone perceived as an authority figure, rest assured that a process of leveling is going on. Cynicism is a dominant attitude. Pastors find themselves caught up in this general trend, mired in the same moods of distrust and suspicion as other professional people. Yet because pastors represent such high ideals and principles, the loss of respect and trust in this quarter presents a more pitiable plight.

Perfectly good people enter the ministry year after year; I watch them graduate and accept their first call or appointment. Into that setting they take their sense of calling from God, their high ideals and personal standards, and their expectations that God will lead them through the rest of their lives. Their faith has survived the test of seminary courses and increasingly complicated denominational ordination processes. Yet something happens during their practice of pastoral ministry that produces a crisis. They seem to lose a sense of who they are in the process of trying to be good pastors.

I believe the solution to this identity crisis does not lie with changes made by individual pastors, although changes anywhere will help. The problem is more systemic: It involves the very nature of ordained ministry as practiced today. To reach genuine resolution, we need to come to some understanding of pastoral ministry as vocation.

I believe spiritual guidance can serve as *the* organizing principle for ministry. I apply the central image of the pastor as spiritual guide to the various functions of ministry: worship leading, pastoral care, teaching, social change, and administration. Our learnings from the emerging discipline of spiritual direction can inform and rescue the work of ministry. Spiritual guidance as a metaphor for ministry provides a unique and valuable pastoral focus.

My prayerful hope is that both clergy and laypersons will find this book helpful as they work together to transform the church from a highly secularized institution into the beloved community, which is the body of Christ. Pastors alone cannot do this; the people with whom they work need to have shared expectations and a shared vision. Without church members' support, no pastor can make the necessary changes in the practice of his or her calling. I never could have written this book without my own experience in the congregations that have shaped me over the years: First Presbyterian Church of Marshfield, Wisconsin, my home congregation, where the seeds of faith were planted, and House of Faith Presbyterian Church of Minneapolis, Minnesota, my first pastorate after seminary where I learned what ministry meant. The people of this congregation allowed me to try my hand at ministry and allowed me to make mistakes. They forgave me many times, thus encouraging me to grow. Emmanuel Presbyterian Church of Chicago was the setting where my skills for ministry were tempered in the fires of the inner city and honed and blessed by the lives of those who met and loved me. First Presbyterian

Church of San Anselmo, California, is the place that welcomed and included my family and me after I joined the faculty of San Francisco Theological Seminary.

Seventh Avenue Presbyterian Church of San Francisco, where I serve as a Parish Associate, is the setting of a wonderful diversity of God's people and has been a source of constant inspiration through the years. Sleepy Hollow Presbyterian Church of San Anselmo, where my wife, Nancy, and I worshiped for several years is the setting for a birthing of a new form of congregational life and worship among people largely unchurched and under the age of fifty. Church of the Roses, where we now worship and where I presently serve as Theologian in Residence, is a gracious and welcoming congregation that has taken us in and made us feel that we belong.

Each of these congregations has taught me something about the meaning of ministry. Each of them has contributed to this book. In addition, students and graduates of San Francisco Theological Seminary have contributed to my understanding of the issues facing pastors today. They have taught me while I have been teaching them. I especially want to thank Nicola Frail, a student at San Francisco Theological Seminary, who assisted me in this project by doing research to determine the accuracy of the quotations used. I am deeply indebted to George Donigian and Rita Collett of Upper Room Books for encouragement and wonderful editorial assistance.

CHAPTER ONE

A Calling Seeking Definition

IN TIMES OF CONFUSION about the nature and mission of the church such as those in which we live today, the work of ministry is not easily defined. Different people understand ministry in different ways; congregations disagree widely on the issue of what to expect from a pastor. A single congregation contains persons of widely differing views and expectations. Pastors often get caught in this conflict of expectations: If they satisfy one definition of ministry, they may alienate those with a different definition.

Pastors themselves bring different understandings to the work of ministry. Many pastors have inherited certain images of ministry from role models. Many of us carry our seminary faculty members with us into our ministry. I know I preached with my Old Testament professor looking over my shoulder for several years; in my mind, he was checking to see that my exegesis was sound. Other images of ministry come from books we have read. Sometimes books about the ministry become just one more difficult burden that critiques who we are and what we do. These varying and competing demands can tear the pastor apart; it is impossible to satisfy all of the expectations.

One way to find clarity about the work of the ministry is to examine the church's self-definition, to ask the church what it believes is its reason for being. The work of pastoral ministry is always closely connected to the ministry of the whole people of God. The principal task of those set apart by ordination for pastoral ministry is "to equip the saints for the work of ministry, for building up the body of Christ" (Eph. 4:12). Because the work of ordained ministry is in service of the church, we cannot understand that work apart from contemporary ecclesiology. The church's self-understanding will always impact the nature of pastoral ministry. Clergy provide the core leadership of every congregation; the leadership provided by ordained pastors is for the purpose of guiding the congregation in fulfilling its own mission of making disciples of Jesus Christ.

Mission and self-understanding are bound together mutually. Any separation of the ministry of the church from the work of the ordained leads to confusion within the body of Christ. Such confusion may lead to competition and possible conflict between leaders and people, which can destroy the whole body. If the people do not share the pastor's understanding of the church, the potential for struggle and warfare will loom large between them.

In its wisdom, the church has recognized that ministry needs to be defined in such a way that the work of leaders is commonly understood. Churches have persisted throughout history in holding up a central image for the work of ministry that expresses in each age the core meaning of ministry for both the pastoral leaders and for the people. To understand the central image, or metaphor, for ministry is to grasp the inherent problems and the potential resources for doing ministry.

Over the centuries, the organizing principle and thus the central image for ordained ministry has changed—sometimes quite dramatically and drastically. This change reflects shifts in the societal position of the minister, the setting of the church in its particular culture, and the general expectation of churches about themselves.

IMAGES OF MINISTRY FROM CHURCH HISTORY

The New Testament evidences several different forms of ministry because the church had not fixed upon definite organizational forms. Women as well as men shared in ministry as they had shared in ministry with Jesus and his disciples. Ordination arose only after a period of time in which the sole qualification for leadership was the action of the Holy Spirit. The leader expressed the gift of the Spirit in a way that benefited the whole community. The first image for Christian ministry was that of one gifted with spiritual power. That power issued forth in preaching, teaching, speaking in tongues, healing, and, above all, evangelizing. While the Christian church was struggling to convert Gentiles and to become an organized entity, the *pastor as evangelist* served as an important model for ministry.

By the early Middle Ages, the central metaphor for pastoral ministry had become the *pastor as mediator of sacramental grace.* The church had come to believe that only men were qualified for ordination because Jesus was a man. The pastor interceded between the people and God and held the keys to the kingdom by virtue of ordination. The pastor gave expression to those keys through the power of the sacraments. Only pastors could offer forgiveness in the sacrament of penance, and only pastors could effect the miracle of the mass and provide people with the bread of life. Pastors could preclude people from receiving God's grace, or pastors could open that grace to all. Church members may or may not have liked their pastors, but they did not anger or oppose them. Their fear both of the pastor's possible power to harm as well as to bless brought respect.

The Protestant Reformation of the sixteenth and seventeenth centuries produced a dramatic change in this early central metaphor for ordained ministry. With the Reformation, the pastor became the one who proclaimed the good news to the people. The guiding principle for ministry became that of *preacher*. The invention of the printing press and the increased literacy of the general population added weight to the centrality of preaching of scripture as the model for pastoral ministry. As Protestant pastors fulfilled this definition of ministry, they still were endowed with divine authority, but the authority stemmed from their knowledge of the scriptures. When pastors ascended into the pulpits, they became more than orators; people paid close attention because they interpreted scripture. Without exaggeration, it has been said that preaching was the third sacrament of the Reformation. Preachers were understood to speak for God, and people earnestly pursued right hearing. Protestant pastors were no less powerful than Roman Catholic priests.

The Protestant principle of open access to the Bible, which gave the people the right to read and interpret the scriptures themselves, modified pastoral power somewhat. The people could disagree with their pastors, and they did so—often quite vigorously. The pastor as preacher never inspired the awe given to the pastor as the sacramental mediator of grace. Parishioners who read their Bibles could come to different conclusions than their pastors. They might become persuaded that their pastors were unfaithful to scripture, and they could oppose their pastors. Among Protestants, sacramental ministry occupied a place below the function of preaching.

The pastor as preacher became the conscience of the community, the ethical guide who enforced the upholding of God's values and required consistency of community values with stated theology and scripture. The pastor served as the resident theologian who interpreted the faith to the people, helping them make sense of the biblical faith tradition by applying the teaching to their lives. Rather than dispensing grace, the pastor opened the doorway to grace, enabling the people to encounter grace for themselves.

The difference between the central images of pastor as preacher and pastor as mediator of sacramental grace is not as dramatic as Protestants have thought. Both Word and sacrament are mediating forms of ordained ministry; both place the pastor between God and the congregation. Both Word and sacrament are forms of divine accommodation to human limitation and weakness. We cannot grasp God's mystery until that mystery is mediated to us in some form that we can understand. Both Word and sacrament offer means that enable us to grasp the otherwise inscrutable; both represent divine disclosure. The person who stands before the people as keeper of the sacraments or as the preacher and interpreter of God's will has great power, rooted in the understanding of the role as intermediary between the people and God. Both Word and sacrament are means of God's self-accommodation to our human situation, and those who preach and celebrate sacraments come to represent God's power.

In many parts of the world and in many different faith communities within the United States (particularly among African Americans, Hispanics, and Koreans) the pastoral role still carries power. The metaphor of the pastor as preacher still commands respect. Whenever the preaching role is central, the pastor is likely to have more power. The power of preaching often becomes the power to represent the community of faith in the larger community, to serve as the spokesperson for the people, to be the voice of the voiceless.

Dr. Martin Luther King Jr. was an excellent example of a pastor who understood and used the power of the pulpit to change the social climate beyond the boundaries of a single congregation. What King personified in the mid-twentieth century on a national scale was once quite ordinary on a local level. The pastor articulated the inherent values of society. For people who either could not read or had little access to books or newspapers, the pulpit was the primary source of information about the world. Even if they subscribed to a newspaper, the pastor's words were quoted as news. The pulpit made news. What the pastor preached became the subject of editorials and community discussion. The pulpit shaped society.

The Protestant pastor often was the best-educated person in town, commanding high respect. People spoke in hushed tones, watched their grammar, and avoided off-color remarks in the presence of the "man of God." A good education, the moral power of the pulpit, and an opportunity to reach large numbers of people combined to provide pastors with a good deal of prestige in the community.

The understanding of the pastor's central work as preacher carries implications about the central mission of the church. If preaching is the primary means by which the leader equips the church for its ministry, then persuasion and conviction become the primary tools necessary for the implementation of the ministry that belongs to them all. The people's ability to apply scripture to their lives is critical to their discipleship. They discover their connection to God through the "right" hearing of the Word proclaimed. The church understands itself as an organization faithful to the Word of God. The task of the people becomes that of faithfully hearing and obeying the Word.

IMAGES OF MINISTRY IN THE MODERN CHURCH

Among most mainline Protestants, the growing literacy of parishioners has meant change for the pastor's role. This change began before the turn of the twentieth century and began to accelerate after the First World War. As the population became more educated, more secular, and more worldly wise, the pulpit no longer remained the primary source of information. People did not wait patiently for the following Sunday to hear God's word on a particular subject or even to be informed about the state of the world. Instead, they read editorials in the daily paper or listened to the radio, and they paid far less attention to what the pastor said. Newspapers were less impressed by sermons and cited them far less often than previously. Churches discovered that they had to pay to advertise the title of the coming sermon; and unless the title denoted shocking content in some dramatic way, the news media ignored the content of preaching. People still went to hear sermons, but the preacher did not exercise the kind of power over their lives that was normative in the previous century.

Many pastors became convinced that preaching was no longer important; they lost confidence in themselves. The loss of their primary power, and thus their primary means of self-understanding, brought a significant sense of devaluation to many pastors. Although preaching still exists as a primary means of the exercise of pastoral responsibility and still carries great authority for many people, it is no longer the dominant image for pastoral ministry for many clergy.

The loss of confidence in preaching—both by pastors and by parishioners—produced a subsequent loss of confidence in pastoral ministry. Pastors asked themselves, *What contribution can I actually make?* Because the work of ministry is always difficult to identify, many began to look for a new way to express their understanding of ministry. In an attempt to discover some overall sense of what they had been called to be and do, pastors sought a new central metaphor. This ongoing search for a new central metaphor has engaged many of us who have been in ministry for several decades; the history of this effort is our own history. Our search is an effort to take society seriously as the context for ministry; thus the search itself expresses our desire for relevance. In the search for a new central understanding for the work of the church and the central metaphor for ministry, several options briefly took center stage. Each metaphor offered an important attempt to be faithful to the call of God; each expressed genuine desire to fulfill a call from God. The metaphors did not come in any fixed order; different pastors discovered them in different times. The following order is one way of describing the changes, recorded in the order of my own experience.

Education

Some pastors turned to the newly developing work of professional educators. They became experts in educational theory and developed ministries that focused on teaching. They used the most up-to-date teaching methods available. Some went back to school to study under the finest educational theorists. For these pastors, education became the central way to think about the work of ordained ministry.

Denominations that had remained aloof from the developing Sunday school movement throughout the nineteenth and early twentieth centuries suddenly began to take notice. The attention given to education related closely to the boom in births. Most of this growth took place in the years immediately following World War II. In response to the amazing growth in numbers of children, churches developed great new educational programs, and each denomination developed its own curricular materials. These new curricular materials were beautiful and closely graded. They assumed that church school teachers would spend considerable time preparing their lessons. This approach called upon pastors to take an active role in interpreting the teaching task to these lay volunteers.

Congregations replicated the best new public school facilities. These "educational plants" had every educational resource that money could buy to support the determination that church education be high quality. Churches built most of the beautifully equipped educational units in the 1950s and early 1960s. Ironically many of these facilities now sit empty except for the leased space occupied by a preschool.

When pastors and churches understood education as primary for equipping the church for ministry, persons believed teaching the basics of the faith to be the key ingredient for pastoral ministry. Persons perceived biblical illiteracy and theological/historical ignorance as enemies to discipleship. If people could become more knowledgeable about their beliefs, they would become more skilled in the practice of their faith, more self-critical, and more aware of the issues facing Christians in the world. Through teaching, the pastor equipped the people of God for a life of discipleship in the world.

A significant problem for those who conceived of education as the central focus of ministry lay in the parishioners' lack of eager response. Many carefully planned classes were not particularly well received, even when these classes used the best curricular resources available, were held in spaces specially equipped with the latest audiovisual materials, and were taught by pastors who had studied to be the best possible teachers.

People seemed remarkably resistant to learning more about the faith. Those who attended classes often avoided the newly designed courses in church history and theology, preferring the familiar Bible classes that did not use the new materials. Pastors sought explanations for what they experienced as apathy, and many pastors blamed the people for refusing to open themselves to new ideas. But whatever the reason for the resistance, if the people are not present, it is hard to have an active teaching ministry.

Psychology

Other pastors developed interest in the field of psychology. Both the pastoral counseling movement and the education movement began to develop at about the same time, early in the twentieth century. Both of these sciences were developing in secular society, so the church took an interest in these new skills for working with people. Part of faithfulness to the gospel involves the use of current means to communicate the faith.

Some pastors became pastoral counselors exclusively, seeing only clients. A few large congregations developed their own counseling centers and hired a staff of ordained and unordained professionally trained counselors. In some communities, several congregations pooled their resources and established Christian counseling centers, family life centers, or similar centers called by other names. People sought out these trained pastors because they used the language of psychology. Pastoral counselors could speak to people who were not attracted to or comfortable with the language of religion.

Most pastors tried to counsel persons in addition to keeping up their other responsibilities. Time management became more difficult as more and more people sought out those with skills in this area. These pastors discovered that they had less and less time for other pastoral work. Many people seeking pastoral help fell outside the ranks of church membership and had no particular interest in the church. Already busy schedules became unmanageable. Often pastors could add this new focus for ministry only by letting go of or reducing time spent on pastoral visitation, teaching, or sermon preparation. Not surprisingly, many congregants became unhappy with their pastors.

Yet the ministry of counseling brought feelings of satisfaction. Pastors who lacked a sense of purpose or importance experienced the ego boost of having people seek them out and solicit their help. I recall how important my counseling made me feel in my first pastorate. I also know that the more people I saw, the more I attracted hurting people into the life of the congregation.

For those engaged in counseling, the psychological metaphor equipped people for ministry by helping individuals overcome barriers to their fulfillment as persons, enabling them to better serve others. Leaders operating out of this metaphor believed that people who got in touch with themselves, who discovered their buried angers and fears, and who learned to accept themselves would be better equipped to act with compassion and love in the world. If individuals could find freedom from personal barriers, they would be better able to choose the path of their own particular discipleship more carefully and wisely, a path that fit their unique personalities and thus had integrity.

Social change

Other pastors turned their attention to their neighborhoods, to see and respond to events outside the walls of the church building. They witnessed tremendous human suffering in society, and the church's inability or unwillingness to be in touch with that pain alarmed and disturbed them. They focused their interest on how institutions and communities change. The idea of the pastor as agent of change became a basic model. To enable the church to become an agent of change for society, pastors studied and applied the principles of community organization and conflict management.

In this role definition, pastors helped equip the church for its ministry by encouraging the church to become an instrument of social change rather than a static defender of the status quo. The church had to win its right to speak for God in a world that needed voices of reason and compassion so people might see and believe and possibly join the pilgrimage. To the degree that the church understood itself in relation to society's problems and saw its role as prophet and reconciler, the church was fulfilling its mission.

Two areas of ministry related to the metaphor of change agent were these: the civil rights movement and opposition to the war in Vietnam. As cities became more troubled, white flight reduced concern for cities on the part of people who moved to the newly created suburbs. Churches and pastors striving to minister in cities and to make their congregations relevant to urban problems such as crime, lack of public services, poverty, and unemployment could not stay removed from the civil rights movement. To care about civil rights demonstrated concern for the people with whom they engaged in ministry. The war in Vietnam also mobilized many pastors to become agents of change. They began to organize students in protest against the policies of the United States government, some because they pastored young people who agonized about how to avoid the draft. Other pastors became involved because they saw that this war was tearing families apart, sometimes even their own families. Pastors with draft-age sons tended to be more involved in the moral issues revolving around the war than others who could maintain more distance from the issues.

Its close identification with these two movements meant that the future of the social change model depended on continued interest and support for these subjects. The interest in Vietnam declined as the war wound down. The assassination of Dr. Martin Luther King Jr. and the rise of the Black Power movement also marked a rapid decline in interest in the civil rights movement on the part of white people. The President did not have close ties to that movement. Americans expressed their weariness with turmoil and their desire for a return to calm.

Richard Nixon's election in 1968 signaled the beginning of the end of the dominant role these two central issues played in society and in community change. During this same time, churches noticed a loss both in members and finances. Those who had been in the forefront of the movement for social change became the scapegoats for membership loss. Denominations that had supported various community organization projects began to back away because they no longer had either the money or the enthusiasm.

Business management

A fairly recent model for pastoral ministry arose in response to the church's failure to find unity in its life and ministry. As conflict over social policy and mission direction tore congregations and denominations apart, a new vision for ministry that was far less strident and more harmonious arose. The new model viewed the pastor as the manager of an institution (the church). The pastor's *study* became the pastor's *office*. This renaming reflected a crucial shift in understanding. As the pulpit and the classroom declined in importance, as people went elsewhere for therapy, and as grand dreams to change the world seemed rather fruitless, pastors began to search for self-authentication and satisfaction through business administration and organizational development.

The theme of the minister as manager was not totally new. H. Richard Niebuhr, writing in 1956, prophetically referred to ministers as "pastoral directors." Niebuhr saw that the primary principle for many pastors already had become that of organizing and managing a complex organization. What Niebuhr foresaw became a reality as denominations urged pastors to study the forms of administration borrowed from the business community which, in turn, had borrowed them from the military. Management by objective (MBO) was incorporated into an understanding of leadership. Entire denominations adopted MBO methods to organize people for ministry. *Planning, budgeting*, and *evaluating* became key words in proclaiming the gospel. The factors promoting this model resided in avoiding unnecessary conflict, getting rid of inefficiency and waste, and focusing on issues according to their priority.

During the predominance of this management emphasis, a "good" pastor's skills included the ability to organize events, to keep several programs going at the same time, to enable leadership development from among the people, and to ensure proper development of a budget that used standard accounting procedures and practices.

Nothing is wrong with these goals. Without their accomplishment, chaos might result. Yet something was missing. In this model, one could only envision what was doable; plans needed to be realistic and not "pie in the sky." In fact, realism sounded the primary note. Yet the management skills intended to free pastors from duplicated effort and to provide church people with means to do their work more democratically and effectively produced a sense of loss—the loss of vision.

Despite great effort to persuade pastors of the value of the management metaphor both to pastors and congregations, it just never took hold. Styles of management theory didn't stir pastors' imaginations. Although clergy attended the classes set up for them by denominational organizations, this conceptualization of the work of ministry did not generate enthusiasm among the pastors.

Ministers and congregations found it hard to grasp the vision of the management model for ministry. The spoken vision of the church as a smoothly running institution could not satisfy anyone as a central model for ministry. Ultimately the lack of a real vision for this model is what kept the movement from wide acceptance. Pastors grew bored with protracted procedures that seemed to go nowhere. The metaphor offered no dramatic or compelling vision for the church. A significant problem with management as a model for ministry was that few pastors implemented this kind of ministry well. Neither their hearts nor their education contributed to their skill in this kind of management.

THE IMPORTANCE OF A NEW DEFINING IMAGE

Teaching, educating, counseling, acting for societal change, and managing the organization fall within an overall understanding of ministry. Each has its place in any understanding of the work of ministry. They all belong! The problems these models encountered arose from their dependence on a secular discipline for support. In the effort to become relevant to the contemporary view of human life, they included many important perspectives but did not build on a theological base. Perhaps because the traditional work of ordained ministry shifted as society changed, pastors and denominations felt pressured to look elsewhere for answers. H. Richard Niebuhr wrote the following words:

> Great discussions developed over the question how to make the gospel relevant to needs it never had had primarily in view. It was translated into evolutionary and social terms, though it resisted efforts to cast it into such strange forms. Confusion was bound to result. The political needs of [people] struggling for survival or status, the economic needs of hungry and competitive [people], the psychological needs of anxious and guilty interpersonal beings, these and other highly important wants seemed to require the ministrations of the Church. And to justify themselves churches and ministers had before them the example of the Great Physician and Reformer who had compassion on every [one] in natural need and prophesied to an oppressed, divided nation threatened by disaster. The context in which he did these things, the cause for which he came out and why he was sent was often forgotten.[1]

Each of these central images for pastoral ministry displays a basic lack of confidence in the ordained ministry as a unique and definable calling with its own methods, its own tools, and its own intrinsic worth. Each also suggests that clergy do not think they have anything to offer that society needs or wants.

RETURNING TO A BASIC IMAGE

When people turn to a pastor, what are they seeking? Whatever their response, they are looking for a source of validity in their lives. They are looking for a model of being in the world that is anchored in God. They seek, sometimes with near desperation, someone who can point them toward depth and meaning. They turn to their pastors in the hope that they will find someone who will suffer with them in their struggles and rejoice with them in their recurring discovery of God's unexpected presence.

People turn to a doctor because they believe a doctor can help them get well. They visit a dentist because they have a toothache or because they need an annual dental checkup. To build a house, people call upon the services of an architect, engineer, or carpenter. To learn Spanish, one goes to someone who teaches Spanish. Most professional people serve a clear and well-defined purpose.

Such clear-cut purposes do not always exist for those who turn to their pastors. They may be unable to articulate what they seek from a pastor. They may be unable to express their own deepest longings; yet these very longings are central to their search when they choose to visit a pastor instead of a psychologist or a teacher or a doctor. They may call upon a pastor because life no longer works for them. In their sense of failure, they may decide that life ought to include a larger place for God.

Henri J. M. Nouwen wrote, "If it is possible for a doctor to cure a patient even where the doctor hardly believes in the value of life, a minister will never be able to be a minister if it is not his [or her] own most personal faith and insight into life that forms the core of pastoral work."[2] That central insight is key to the issue of the pastor's role. Persons in other professions can depend upon particular tools of the trade or upon skills learned in professional school to get them by—even when they have ceased to care very much or believe very much in what they are doing. But the principal tool of pastors is not a particular skill or technique; it is our very being. The principal tool for the work of pastoral ministry is one's own faith.

Pastors who have genuine and mature faith will have something to say to the troubled souls who seek them out to hear them preach or to request their counsel. Pastors who have faith can respond with tenderness and wisdom; they do not have to pretend to have all the answers or even to have more information than their parishioners. Pastors with genuine faith can meet the need presented by the person who really wants that intangible something we might call a "sense of God" in his or her life.

Equipping the church for ministry involves helping people individually and corporately develop a healthy, balanced, and appropriate faith. Such a faith will provide the context where they may express themselves in healthy action on behalf of others. Marcus J. Borg in *Jesus: A New Vision* articulates the twin aches of modern people: "cosmic loneliness" and "a yawning sense of meaninglessness." Only the pastor can help persons find deliverance from these aches. Stable physical and emotional health, relevance to the social setting, legal aid, nice teeth, proper diet, exercise, and good marriages will not by themselves answer people's needs to discover a friendly God at the center of the universe. Many of the good things that we highly and properly value do not enable people to discover meaning in the ordinary events of life. The ability to assist people toward development of a faith that can celebrate and connect with the mystery at the center of all creation and name that mystery as the God of love is the central service that pastors offer to persons. Pastors are called to offer this unique gift of naming and celebrating to persons in the community of faith.

Ministerial competence is important. Pastors must possess some gifts that they can develop into real abilities in order to serve the church. But abilities themselves are not the primary gifts pastors have to offer. Abilities do not form the basis for ministry. We can get caught up easily in the effort to validate our ministry by results. Success can become an idol to which we cling in order to keep going. Frequently when groups of pastors get together, one hears success stories told as evidence of the validity of persons' ministry and identity.

People may ascribe to pastors a more priestly role than is theologically correct. Church members believe their pastors are people who know God, who have a deep and personal relationship with God as evidenced in a life of prayer. These parishioners may ask a pastor to pray at times when they could just as easily pray themselves. They really hope that God hears the pastor's prayers because they think God may not hear their own, or they fear they do not have the right words.

Because people know that the experience of God's nearness can bring both distress and power, their relationship with God is always somewhat ambiguous. While drawn to that relationship, they resist. While seeking a closer sense of God, they want to keep God at a safe and comfortable distance. Their very ambivalence about God leads them to seek spiritual leaders who can mediate the Holy. They look for pastors who can serve as trustworthy guides, pastors who can stand somewhat apart from their lives of struggle and point them toward that which they both seek and resist.

Rather than running away from these expectations, a healthier approach might come in pastors' recognizing the priestly expectation as real and legitimate. The opposite danger resides in pastors' eager acceptance of the role. This acceptance may result in our straining ourselves to become what we think we should be, distancing ourselves from our own real needs. This leads to pretense and hypocritical actions.

Instead of running from people's expectations or leading a life of pretense, a pastor can live as one who dares to be a person for others. Nouwen put it this way: "Ministry means the ongoing attempt to put one's own search for God with all the moments of pain and joy, despair and hope, at the disposal of those who want to join the search but do not know how."[3] One might quibble with this definition. After all, it is not so much a matter of *our* search for God as it is our finding the God who is searching for us. But in our human experience, it feels as if we are looking for God in a world where God does not always appear to be obvious. Nouwen hit upon a central metaphor for ministry: The pastor is the guide to the spiritual life. No better definition for the work of ministry exists than this: to put one's own search for God at the disposal of others. Such an action suggests a new vision for the work of the church.

Our society hungers for spiritual connection. People turn to many different sources for the assurance of God's presence, for an understanding of their relationship to God, and for ways of developing sensitivity to their personal experiences. The church can be a place that nurtures human souls, a place that meets people's basic hunger for God, and a place that nourishes the people of God in their ministry as those who understand themselves in relationship to God. Pastors as spiritual guides can lead in the church's revitalization as it struggles to become the institution it needs to be to meet the human longing that seeks for more than correct answers or moral guidance. The hunger that draws people to cults, New Age experimentation, or the occult is the hunger for God that is primary in our age. People either will be drawn to the church to meet their need for God, or they will look elsewhere.

I invite all of us who would be of help to those who earnestly seek God to consider the metaphor of spiritual guidance for our work. We have a unique calling to be a spiritual guide. We will meet a genuine need, and we will play an important role in the lives of people by doing that for which our own calling, life experience, and training uniquely qualify us.

CHAPTER TWO

The Spiritual Context for Pastoral Ministry Today

M ANY PEOPLE in our culture are seeking answers to their questions of ultimacy with near desperation. They want to know the eternal meaning of their lives; they fear that all they have worked to achieve has no real meaning no matter how well they have done. Many otherwise successful people are dissatisfied with the material rewards of Western culture because they feel empty inside. Despite their achievements and possessions, they feel a sense of incompleteness. They have no sense of purpose greater than getting by, doing well, accumulating possessions, and living as long as possible without pain. Such goals, while not wrong, will not sustain their souls; and those people who have no greater goals tend to exist in a permanent sense of dissatisfaction.

This unease often expresses itself in the willingness of some people to follow any guru who promises to assuage their ache for eternity. These desperate people will give up everything in order to be with their leader and to gain acceptance and a sense of belonging. The same kind of need is also present in those people who remain dissatisfied but stuck in the ruts of their material existence: unhappy, perhaps bitter, unwilling to change. For some reason they are unwilling to trust what they cannot see or prove.

Part of the New Age movement's appeal is that it offers people a way of getting in touch with the eternal. It offers a means of bridging the gulf between their ordinary lives and the mystery that underlies everything that is, the mystery called God. Some of the people most concerned about pursuing a relationship with God have left organized religion because they have sensed that churches, despite all their language, have no real spiritual depth. They have joined the host of those who believe without belonging, who see the structures of institutional religion as impediments to their spiritual pilgrimage. They cannot imagine that concern about the details of carpet color, budget distribution, struggles for power among various groups, or conflicts about the frequency of Communion are necessary for their spiritual lives. We are tempted to criticize them for their shallowness, their fickleness, or their lack of grounding. Those of us in the institutional church must temper our criticism of these new believers, for they are fellow pilgrims searching for God.

Whatever the belief system, the primary anxiety of most Americans is that of meaninglessness: Life does not make sense, and nothing can mask the terrible anxiety that such a lack creates. The scientific worldview of enlightened rationalism does not serve well in a world where things seem to be falling into chaos. Since the eighteenth century, the Enlightenment worldview has promised that more knowledge and more research could solve every problem and cure every illness. The heart of the rational worldview rests on logic, reason, and predictability. Rationalism prevents people from recognizing the mysteries present in their lives. Operating from this worldview, persons interpret every unexplained event as something about which we do not yet have answers; with more knowledge and more time, we will understand and the mystery will disappear. At one point in my own education, I believed that a miracle was nothing more than an event for which I had no information to provide a rational explanation. Inevitably, Western thinking has developed a secular attitude that allows very little place for God.

Today people are observing and mourning the absence of God, evidenced by the renewal of interest in spirituality. All of us experience puzzling events, hints of eternity in the midst of our mortality. What we cannot understand or explain may threaten us. We cannot control mystery; it just happens. Many of us have found it necessary to use the term *coincidence* to describe an event that others might describe as a miracle. A secular worldview finds it less threatening to acknowledge a coincidence than any form of divine intervention.

Even those who attend church feel a sense of loss—perhaps not the loss of God—a sense that life is flat and meaningless. The routines of organized religion no longer satisfy many who are discontent with a faith that is correct, obedient, and intellectually demanding but lacking soul. A host of burned-out church members and pastors have grown cynical in the process of doing good. They bear witness to the human need for something more than duty. Some former churchgoers have joined nonmembers in a general movement to recapture the meaning of mystery, an appreciation of the spiritual power that comes to human beings from beyond them. They have left the church to engage in their spiritual quest, a search for God.

Spirituality names the process of searching for a vital relationship to God. While taking many forms, this search basically describes the experience of Western society today. People are awakening to a sense of their own need for God. This awakening causes them to affirm their creatureliness, created by God and meant for relationship with God. This affirmation leads them to realize they are less than human without that relationship.

Some scholars think we are living in a time of religious revival and refer to this as a new awakening. The large sale of books on the spiritual life and the popularity of courses on the inner life reinforce that view. Even public opinion surveys point to this strong interest in a meaningful relationship with God. Polls indicate that Americans are unshakable believers in God: Americans pray and expect that God will answer; Americans also believe in life after death. However, these beliefs do not lead to Christian discipleship or church membership. The religious expression remains personal and individual; institutions, particularly those of organized religion, generate anxiety.

THE CONGREGATION AND THE SPIRITUAL GUIDE

One can understand the life of faith as a pilgrimage toward God. The pilgrimage has a beginning and an end; yet it differs for each person. Part of the task of any spiritual guide is to recognize human uniqueness and thus to respect and value each person's particular pilgrimage. Every effort to force people into a mold of uniformity signals danger: the danger of the cult. The disturbing nature of cults resides in its frightening uniformity. People strain themselves to pretend that they are something they are not. Everyone is trying hard to be like everyone else; everyone is trying hard to be like the leader.

A congregation is not a cult; it is made up of people who are quite different. The pastor, the spiritual guide of the congregation, has the responsibility to guide real people—people with unique stories and special and varied journeys. Central to spiritual guidance is the hard work of attending reverently to the way in which each person has come to terms with God's call and how each has experienced and responded to that call.

Each person begins the pilgrimage in a different way. Some people begin their life of faith with birth and baptism as infants. They always have known themselves as beloved by God; for them Jesus Christ has always been a friend. They have seldom sensed God's absence. The spiritual journey for such people is a steady and consistent development of their sense of God's reality. They may have found it necessary to reclaim and reform their childhood faith in adolescence or to put childhood language into new language to fit their adult experience. Their faith pilgrimage is not a matter of discovering faith but of renewing the gift already present.

These people are like Timothy, to whom the apostle wrote, "I am reminded of your sincere faith, a faith that lived first in your grandmother Lois and your mother Eunice and now, I am sure, lives in you. For this reason I remind you to rekindle the gift of God that is within you" (2 Tim. 1:5-6). The denominations that practice infant baptism reinforce the character of faith as a gift given in infancy. Those of us who began our Christian lives with the seal of baptism as babies know many things from the beginning: our inclusion in God's covenant, Jesus as friend, and God's love for us. The church at its best gives us early childhood memories that assure us of our place in God's world.

We "once borns" have not had a conversion experience because we have not needed one. Our lives have moved steadily in the direction of a maturing, healthy spirituality. We make important discoveries about ourselves; we explore new metaphors for God; and we discover new ways to express our discipleship. We do not start from scratch. Faithfulness may not come easy for us, but our struggles are not desperate life-and-death matters. We continue to find ourselves within the bosom of faith;

we are stretched, sometimes painfully, but the stretching is from a recognizable source: the God we have always known. We search for a deeper, fuller understanding of that God.

Other people either have been born into a secular world or have wandered into that world after rejecting their parents' faith. They find themselves without God, without faith, and without the assurance that their lives matter ultimately. In their inner emptiness, they may identify with Paul who had to be turned from one way of life to another in a dramatic way: "Now as he was going along and approaching Damascus, suddenly a light from heaven flashed around him. He fell to the ground and heard a voice saying to him, 'Saul, Saul, why do you persecute me?'" (Acts 9:3-4). Saul's dramatic turnabout is similar to that of many people in all ages. Their pilgrimage is marked by a moment of insight, a dramatic turn, a time of clarity and assurance—a day they remember all their lives. These "twice-born" people speak about their conversion as such an occasion. Their awareness of the power of that moment, that insight, that turning remains with them vividly. The rest of their days they seek to explore the meaning of that experience of clarity when faith seemed completely obvious. The memory of their conversion is a source of ongoing assurance as they face hardship and doubts along the way. Often the "twice born" have an unshakable confidence based on their memory of their conversion experience.

Although these two Christian experiences differ greatly, persons of both experiences engage in a pilgrimage of seeking to deepen their relationship to God, to enhance their sense of intimacy with God, to renew their commitment as disciples. Whether born into faith or coming to faith as a result of a dramatic experience, every person must discover the necessary process of spiritual growth. The "once born" sometimes envy those who can point to a dramatic moment of encounter with God; yet these need to recognize that the gradual development of faith from childhood is not a curse but a blessing. The goal of both types of experience is the development of trust in Jesus Christ, an ever-growing confidence in God's love, and a sense of relief from the burdens of guilt and the wounds of hurt.

All people experience disturbing events in life, events that challenge even the most mature faith. These challenges necessitate the development of a richer spiritual life. Whether born into faith or recently arrived converts, Christians cannot take their faith journey for granted without danger to the soul. If we are not growing in our faith, we may discover that faith has grown dim, that God has become distant and unreal. The gift of faith has to be kept alive. A chief pastoral task is to assist people in the ongoing renewal of their faith.

FAITH AND GUIDANCE

From biblical beginnings, Christians have identified two parts or stages of the Christian life. First: justification by faith in Christ. God does the saving work for us without our asking or deserving it. God calls us, sometimes getting our attention in dramatic ways, sometimes causing us to pay attention to life's ordinary events. We begin to notice God's presence and love. God's grace precedes all that we can do. God searches for us even before our awareness of our need for God. Without that underlying grace, no one would be interested in pursuing the life of faith. We can recognize God's presence in people's desire for a more spiritual life.

God loves humanity. That is the basic message of the Bible, a message of grace. Justification by faith is God's action to treat us as if we were not sinners. God, in Jesus Christ, opens the way for our restoration to our created humanity. God forgives us before we do anything to deserve that forgiveness. God loves us while we are actively rebelling against God.

The grace of justification by faith prevents people from thinking of life as a do-it-yourself project. Whenever a person forgets that grace is the basis for the life of faith, that person is likely to be self-congratulatory. The human tendency toward sin expresses itself in terrible ways when self-righteousness forms its base. Every person needs a regular reminder that whatever goodness any of us has is a gift of God's love, not proof of our worthiness, goodness, or hard work.

Only after we have recognized God's central part in planting the seed of faith can we begin to follow that second stage of the Christian life: *sanctification* is the part of the faith journey for which we can and must take responsibility. Although grace is free, we may not be predisposed to receive grace without some effort on our part. We make ourselves available to grace in order for God to plant the seed of faith that will take root and grow in us. Any effort on our part is nothing more than a grateful response to what God has done already on our behalf. The person who understands God's love and grace wants to express gratitude for God's blessings and thus seeks to develop thankful patterns for life.

MANY GIFTS, MANY EXPERIENCES

Sanctification will, of course, take different forms in different people. Some people think of the life of faith as relatively easy. A sense of God's graciousness fills these spiritual optimists: In their experience, God answers their prayers consistently, or changes their desires. Prayer is natural for such people; and despite some dark days of difficult faith, their upbeat attitude prevails. Believing comes naturally for them; it fits their personality. These people need little help along the way; the power of the Holy Spirit propels them. Other people may have difficulty handling the enthusiasm and high energy of the spiritual optimists. The optimists may present equal difficulty by appearing smug in their faith. Their greatest temptation may be that of self-righteousness: looking down upon those whose faith journeys may be more of a struggle.

Many other people have a hard time being spiritual. They struggle regularly with issues of doubt. Their prayer efforts at times seem futile. These people feel tempted to give up. A sense of God's absence fills them. These spiritual pessimists desperately need help to sustain them on their journey. They need encouragement, support, and prayer to dispel the doubt and discouragement. Every pastor knows these people well, for they often seek out their pastor's encouragement and prayer. They know their need.

A large number of people fall between these two extremes. These people may have periods of ecstasy and a sense of God's nearness as well as periods of dark despair. Their lives bear witness to signs of God's presence as well as to painful signs of God's absence. They pray and read their Bibles, often finding consolation and spiritual nurture. But they also find the Bible frustrating, dry, and boring. They discover the depth of their own faith; but they also struggle with temptations, doubts, and fears. At times they recognize they cannot make it in life on their own.

Pastors must develop a flexible style of spiritual guidance that allows them to meet the needs of different people, depending upon each person's spiritual disposition. Those who are optimistic may need grounding in the hard realities of the world. They may need reminding of life's difficulty for those whose prayers have not produced easy results. One needs only to point out the poor and oppressed believers of the world who do not escape life's tragedies.

The pessimists require support and encouragement lest they give in to the despair of hopelessness. They need another to uphold them in prayer when they find prayer difficult. They need someone who can sustain belief when they feel only doubt.

The spiritual life is not easy for most people in the modern world. We are overly busy; our lives are filled with noise and activity, and we have a hard time setting aside time for God. We become distracted by the need for attention and approval. Instead of a focus upon God, the spiritual life becomes a parade of piety before others. Jesus repeatedly warned of this temptation. In an age when instant gratification is normative, the spiritual life may seem devoid of positive results.

A sense of God's presence does not just happen for most people. Cultivation of an openness to God is necessary to enable most people to pay attention. Some days it seems that every person engaged in the pilgrimage may feel as if he or she is going backward. Doubts do not disappear easily, and prayer is hard. For this reason, the spiritual life cannot be a do-it-yourself project. Each of us needs companions along the way to offer their help when we cannot help ourselves. We need people who will hold us in prayer when we cannot pray, people whose faith will sustain us in our doubts.

Spirituality is the shape each person gives to the search for intimacy with God in his or her life. Our intentionality determines that shape—those regular practices that help us on our spiritual pilgrimage. Intentionality also implies that we avoid those behaviors or activities that hinder our sense of intimacy with God. No one can develop the life of faith without making choices about the way he or she lives.

All persons need guidance along the spiritual journey.

Without guidance some may easily distort the journey, turning it into a new form of legalism rather than the gracious life God offers. Other thoughtful persons quite rightly want to avoid an imposed discipline that might violate a sense of self. We resist every form of discipline that seems alien and find ourselves with a helter-skelter spiritual life in which we have great intentions but few results. Yet we all need help to avoid the temptations to neglect the spiritual life or to abuse God's gifts. Without some form of caring self-discipline, all of us are subject to the latest fad or at the mercy of the most popular guru. Discipline keeps us open to the ways of God. The disciplines of the Christian life enable people to keep the doors of their hearts open to the One who knocks gently and seeks entrance.

The culture we live in does not value any form of discipline; the very idea of discipline has a bad name. Discipline suggests a rigid set of rules imposed by someone who has power over others. Discipline implies that each of us may be unable to do everything that we want to do or to have everything that we want to possess. Just hearing the word *discipline* prepares one to be lectured at or to be scolded about mistakes or bad habits.

Our society teems with ex-church members who have fled high-handed authority, demanding rules, and rigid expectations. They have rejected forms of religion that define spiritual status by how carefully or correctly one follows the rules. Although some people find temporary solace in being told what to think and how to act, many people find such forms of religion destructive and self-defeating. Ultimately they find that they hear bad news about themselves and their inadequacies rather than good news. Those who seek to measure up to the rules often find that they participate in a pecking order of goodness. The growing number of persons attracted to legalistic preachers and congregations suggests that this ranking has a certain appeal. However, many others leave these same congregations by the back door. The memory of spiritual abuse may deeply scar these exbelievers, which may keep them from further exploration of the spiritual path.

Legalism has an ugly religious history. Self-righteous judgment and domination often have been the primary means of enforcing "proper" behavior or getting people to live up to set standards. Discipline can put the brakes on our enjoyment of life; it can mean going around with a grim sense of duty.

Yet the rudderless condition of modern life has led to a sense of moral and spiritual confusion. All spirituality is a matter both of letting go of hindrances and of taking on practices that nurture the human spirit. Without discipline, the spiritual life collapses in the pressure of the moment or gets pushed aside by the urgent demands of work, family, and culture.

To develop any genuine form of spirituality, we must distance ourselves from a materialistic mindset that discounts everything not available to the senses. Creating space and openness to the Spirit requires an anticipation of a dimension of reality beyond what we can see and touch. Openness to God necessitates distancing ourselves from a culture that expresses its desperate need for control through compulsive activity. Much of life's frantic pace arises from the unceasing effort to keep up the pretense of control. As long as we can keep up the pretense, we feel we are successful. Yet as we grow older, we experience occasions when we know we are not in control, when life goes wrong despite our best efforts.

MEANS OF GRACE

For three centuries, the traditional "means of grace" have provided guidance for Protestant Christians. The means of grace are spiritual disciplines that enable the development and main-tenance of distinctive Christian identity. These "means" allow us to remain open to God's grace. They nurture spiritual growth and maturity in the life of a person or community. They help clear away blocks to God that every person puts up, often unconsciously. The pastor as spiritual guide needs an appreci-ation of these means for the sustenance of the spiritual life. Part of the ministry of spiritual guidance is to suggest these disci-plines as an aid to faith development while implementing them.

1 *Prayer* is the first means of grace and is basic to the Chris-tian life. In prayer, we hold all that we know about our-selves before all that we know about God. We cannot hide anything from God without being false to ourselves. Yet for many people, prayer does not seem to come easily or naturally. Some people pray best when using a book of prayers, reading the prayers of others. In a great prayer from tradition, one can find words to express one's own feelings. Written prayers can become a means to carry one's own thoughts, a wonderful aid when going through a dark time and the right words just do not come. Daily devotional guides to prayer persist in popular-ity because they answer a real need.

Some people find written prayers off-putting—wooden and artificial. These people prefer to pray extemporaneously, out of their own hearts. Still others find that words are not the best way for them to pray. They prefer to pray in silence, sim-ply being in God's presence.

There is no single right way to pray. What is important is that each person discover the style of prayer that fits best, the one that enables the person to practice prayer. Persons who try to pray in a manner that is alien to their spiritual nature will find prayer difficult. One of the tasks of the spiritual guide is to suggest different methods of prayer to those who find their current prayer life unsatisfactory. Pastors must move beyond simply urging people to pray. Scolding the people or even speaking about the importance of prayer can do nothing more than make them feel guilty without making any change in their spiritual lives. Instead, pastors can provide particular models of prayer. Pastors must become teachers of prayer who encourage people by acknowledging that prayer is not easy for everyone. Those for whom prayer is a real struggle can then take heart. Perhaps an assessment of their prayer difficulties reveals the fact that they are trying to pray in a way unsuited to their personality. One pastoral task involves offering prayer options by presenting different ways of praying.

2 *Reading scripture* constitutes a second means of grace. For Protestants especially, but increasingly for Roman Catholics also, the Bible is central for the formation of the spiritual life. Reading scripture is a way of sensing God's nearness and of receiving a direct word from the Lord for one's daily life. Reading the Bible to develop this closeness to God requires a special type of reading in which we 1) read the Bible in small pieces slowly and carefully, attending to the details of the words themselves; and 2) read the Bible prayerfully, expecting that God will speak to us through scripture. As long as we take the Bible for granted or read it only to gain information, we may read the Bible without spiritual benefit. Knowledge of scripture has no particular value if it does not lead us to God. *Lectio divina is a*n ancient tradition of devotional reading of scripture. Norvene Vest provides excellent guidance for this method of spiritual reading. (See the Appendixes, pages 203–6.)

The spiritual guide commends scripture to persons by taking seriously the place of the Bible in preaching and teaching.

If the pastor clearly engages the Bible with dialogue and expectancy, this personal example will encourage parishioners to use that method of reading it for themselves. Teaching the Bible is more than imparting biblical facts; it is helping people recognize the ways the Bible shapes our spiritual journeys.

3 *Meditation* is the third means of grace. Meditation is a form of concentration upon something, a focus upon some word or object that can convey the holy. To meditate means spending time in focused silence. One may meditate upon a text of scripture or other spiritual reading; upon a picture of Jesus; upon an object such as a cross, a lighted candle, or a Bible; or upon some natural object such as a scene of nature, a bird's song, or a sunset. In meditation one practices being quiet, empty, and open to what is present. One stills the soul, quiets the mind, and receives God in whatever form God may choose to be present.

The spiritual guide gives attention to the different ways people find blessing through meditation, gently suggesting and encouraging those forms of meditation compatible with the Christian tradition. The pastor actually may lead classes on meditation in which he or she demonstrates the art of meditation by engaging in it. One learns more easily by doing than by reading about meditation.

4 *Feasting and fasting* is a fourth means of grace. Both withholding food and enjoying food are spiritual disciplines. When fasting, one goes without some good thing for a period of time for the purpose of increasing concentration on prayer. Fasting signals one's true priorities and may help clarify those priorities. One may fast from food, from television, from driving a car, from any activity or thing. We might use the money we save during a time of fasting for a special purpose,

but the fast's purpose is not utilitarian. Fasting offers a time to concentrate on our relationship with God.

Feasting is also a discipline, the discipline of learning to enjoy God's good gifts with gratitude and thankfulness. Cultivation of graceful gratitude may be the single most needed discipline for many people today. Too easily, we take our blessings for granted and even complain about what we do not have. Feasting focuses our concentration on the goodness of our lives, which results in our giving hearty thanks to God.

Both fasting and feasting reflect our relationship with the material world. Every spiritual guide will find it important to help people navigate between extreme world-denying asceticism on the one hand and world-affirming gluttony and greed on the other.

5 *Serving others* is another means of grace. We serve Christ in the presence of others' need. Feeding the hungry, welcoming the homeless, or visiting the sick and those in prison is a spiritual discipline. Being fully present with someone who needs us places us in the presence of the risen Christ. Humble service elevates rather than demeans as we see Christ in the other person.

In going beyond ourselves, we discover that others can use what we have to offer. This meaning, found through serving others, brings blessing to those serving and to those served. An important part of the pastoral task involves providing opportunities for this discovery within the context of the church's mission and ministry. The pastor can make suggestions and provide encouragement and support through preaching and pastoral care to motivate persons' engagement in acts of service.

We also serve others by our financial contributions to meet others' needs. Generosity is a form of spiritual discipline. When we give our money with no strings attached and do not expect gratitude or expressions of thanks, our giving can bless us. Giving generously enough that the gift causes us to have to do without something can be a blessing. When we give without needing to control our gifts but simply let them go in trust, we can be blessed. Humble givers whose giving is an act of faith declare that in giving they receive blessing enough to compensate for whatever sacrifices they have made. Our gifts are ways we can reach out and bless others whom we will never meet personally; they enable us to be a blessing to people far beyond our immediate circle of acquaintances.

6 *Worship* and *sacraments* are obvious means of grace. When we engage in acts of public worship, we place ourselves in the context of grace, submitting ourselves to a setting in which the word is proclaimed and enacted. When we worship, we join other Christians in singing praise. We pray with others and broaden our own concerns beyond the confines of our narrow worlds. Especially in the sacrament of the Lord's Supper, we place ourselves in the presence of the living Christ. In the mystery of the bread broken and the wine poured, we discover that we are made one with Christ.

7 *Holy reading* renews the spiritual life. Many great devotional classics have nurtured people for centuries and continue to benefit us today. Our spirits need materials that will assist them to grow in depth. *The Imitation of Christ* by Thomas à Kempis, *Introduction to the Devout Life* by Frances de Sales, *The Christian Secret of a Happy Life* by Hannah Whitall Smith, *The Pilgrim's Progress* by John Bunyan, and The Chronicles of Narnia series by C. S. Lewis are classics of the spiritual life that one can reread many times in a lifetime.

Church libraries often contain books of this caliber. Their

very presence encourages people to take them home and read them. Churches also might suggest that local booksellers stock the spiritual classics. A pastor's commendation can promote holy reading within the congregation.

8 *Sabbath rest* is making a regular break in the activity of life, moving from doing to resting, from making a living to making a life with God, from taking care of our bodies to tending the needs of our souls. Sabbath keeping is a countercultural activity in a society that has flattened out time so that every day is like another. Society no longer supports the celebration of Sabbath. Modern Americans suffer from diseases caused by stress. People work longer hours than ever before, and a great many people suffer from sleep deprivation. The rhythm of work and rest has disappeared. We all need Sabbath in our lives. We were made for Sabbath rest. When we do not permit ourselves this God-given opportunity to renew our bodies and spirits, we suffer for our neglect of the gift.

For some people, Sabbath may take the form of one day in seven set apart for worship and play. For others, Sabbath may be one week every few months spent in retreat. For still others, Sabbath may come in the form of relaxation and rest an hour or two each day. Every life is different and offers different possibilities for Sabbath; but every person has to have some way of honoring the basic human need for rest and release from the struggle to get ahead. To honor Sabbath is to trust in grace.

We do not have to do it all ourselves. Churches help people honor Sabbath by providing regular opportunities for retreat. Every pastor who tries to guide people's souls will encourage the busiest of them to take time away. Spiritual guides can invite people to take advantage of these retreat opportunities in order to maintain healthier spiritual lives.

WE MAY PRACTICE MOST OF THESE spiritual disciplines both in private and in solitary acts, or we may practice the disciplines in community. In knowing ourselves well, we recognize what works best for us. The church can furnish opportunities to act with and for others, to pray in small groups, and to study scripture with others. Each person also requires the balance of time spent alone in meditation and prayer. A healthy spiritual life balances both solitary and corporate disciplines.

The spiritual guide can help people assert this balance of disciplines in their lives. A guide can recognize signs of withdrawal on the part of those who need to be drawn out of themselves and can notice that being busy is not always a good thing when it serves as a form of escape from something that needs to be faced.

Few disciplines fit into our modern life easily or quickly. Nearly every discipline may feel alien at first. The natural temptation is to give up without really trying. Yet to discover any blessing in them demands practice. Refusing to stay with a discipline that does not produce instant results significantly hinders spiritual growth. God is not a cosmic bellhop. We cannot gain intimacy with God simply by asking for it. One does not develop a spiritual life in a month or a year.

Most of us do not need a new technique so much as we need to practice the disciplines we already know until we fully internalize these disciplines. After being silent for regular periods of time over many months, we may discover that silence is no longer a duty but a blessing. Silence as a part of our life may feel natural and even necessary. When this internalization happens, we recognize it as a gift from God. Disciplines grow slowly and gradually from duty to blessing as they become more natural and as we discover that they assist us in our need.

The discovery of duty-become-blessing may only occur when we get bogged down in old ruts and then remember that our lives feel incomplete without the practice of the very thing we had once thought of as an unwelcome demand. That practice has become a cherished and necessary part of life.

Our remembering that the fruit of any practice is ultimately a gift from God—and not something we achieve on our own—will spare us the terrible anxiety of trying to force ourselves into being persons we were never meant to be. The spiritual life exemplifies an availability to God's gracious presence. We pay attention to the events of our lives so that we see what is really going on, and we discern God's movement in our lives where we might otherwise have seen coincidence or haphazard events without meaning.

As we grow in our relationship, we discover the gracious God who has loved us all along. When we were too busy to notice, God was present. While we struggled to make ourselves acceptable, God loved us. God willed our wholeness when we felt most fragmented. Spiritual discipline is nothing more than a means of learning how to pay attention to God and God's work in our lives.

All of us need spiritual guides. The life of faith is too hard to be lived alone and unaided; the temptations are too great. Each of us needs a guide who will pay attention to us, honor our uniqueness, and demonstrate understanding of our peculiarities. Every spiritual guide has the responsibility to recognize the precious character of each human life. Respect is essential in order to aid persons in their search for intimacy with God. That respect includes our willingness to seek that which is best for the other rather than the satisfaction of being right or of having the other person emulate our way.

CHAPTER THREE

Spiritual Direction as a Metaphor for Ministry

CONSIDER AN EXAMPLE of spiritual guidance from the Bible: the story of Jesus and the Samaritan woman at the well. Jesus violates social and cultural rules by speaking to her; a proper Jew would have avoided a Samaritan and a proper rabbi would have avoided all contact with a woman. Yet Jesus responds to the woman's needs

Jesus encounters her directly by asking for a drink of water. He continues to pay attention to what she says and does, and he tells her the hard truth about herself. He challenges her despite her efforts to turn the conversation in a less personal direction. When Jesus says, "You have had five husbands, and the one you have now is not your husband" (John 4:18), she tries to turn the conversation to institutional practices. Ultimately Jesus turns her life around with his persistent, yet loving, interaction with her. She goes joyfully into the city proclaiming, "Come and see a man who told me everything I have ever done" (John 4:29). In Jesus we meet a master spiritual guide; he paid attention to the disciples, held them in prayer, and spoke truth that enabled their understanding of the real meaning of their lives. The Samaritan woman did not recognize her thirst, but Jesus did. He offered her the living water.

All human beings who care about ultimacy have some questions about God—no matter what they profess about religion. All of us dream perplexing dreams and experience strange events that coincidence cannot adequately explain. Often events come together in ways we could never have imagined possible.

Let's consider that these unexplained events just might be signs of God's presence and involvement in our lives. Such events include the miracles of human love and forgiveness, the beauty of a sunset or a piece of music, sudden and unexplained healing of disease, or the sense of God's immediacy in an ordinary moment—times when God seems real: We clearly sense God's addressing us, and the way ahead seems clear. We can put together the parts of our lives in order to make them whole.

We also may misunderstand or misinterpret those times—at peril to ourselves or others. We have all read newspaper and magazine accounts of someone who has committed a terrible act because "God told me to do it." Misinterpretation of spiritual experience can lead to dangerous situations. In the midst of moments when God is most real and close, we all need help sorting out our experiences and discovering their meaning: Are they signs of God or figments of our imagination?

Yet many people experience times when God seems far away, when life makes no sense, when darkness seems to be the most profound reality. We get discouraged and feel a sense of hopelessness about life. In such times we wonder if our highest aspirations are merely figments of our imagination.

Without help, all of us misunderstand the clues, fill our lives with activity, or allow pain or pleasure to distract from God's presence and activity. Our own efforts to make sense of our experience and to understand our hunger for God sometimes end in bewilderment. Our lack of progress and the seeming confusion of our minds discourage us. No one can grow in grace and love without guidance. There is too much we do not know and cannot comprehend.

When we recognize and understand the difficulty of the spiritual life, we acknowledge our need for the help of another: someone who will listen to us without judgment or attempting to "fix" us, someone wise enough to offer counsel derived from concern for our well-being.

People, rightly or wrongly, assume that their pastor is prepared to deal with their deepest spiritual questions and can provide guidance through the darkness of confusion, doubt, and sense of absence. They expect that their pastor may be the one person to whom they can turn for understanding when they have had a divine encounter, heard a voice speaking in their soul, or experienced a miraculous event. They look for someone who can understand their experience, someone who is on the same journey but just a bit further along. They may seek a spiritual guide in the person of their pastor. The question for the pastor is, What is the best way to be available to persons as they seek guidance for their spiritual journey, and how do I offer such guidance?

SPIRITUAL GUIDANCE AND SPIRITUAL DIRECTION

The relationship of spiritual guidance to spiritual direction is the same as that of pastoral care to therapy. Pastoral care benefits from psychotherapeutic insights and methods and uses therapists for referral. Spiritual guidance is a process of pointing people and groups, small or large, beyond the visible realities to the reality of God as the One without whom we cannot possibly understand our present situation. Guidance uses the insights and skills of spiritual direction and will use trained spiritual directors for referral. Spiritual guidance has a sacramental quality of seeing the work of God in the ordinary. This guidance takes place in the way a leader assists a person, a group, or a congregation to pay attention to the ways God is at work in their lives, individually and corporately. Spiritual guidance is less structured and formal than spiritual direction.

The pastor, as spiritual guide, assists the whole congregation to discover the presence of God in its corporate life. An important part of the task of guidance is to point out signs of that presence. The pastor holds the congregation in prayer and pays close attention to what is taking place. To do this, the pastor must step back from congregational activities. Times of silence for prayer and reflection are important occasions that enable the pastor to discern what might otherwise escape notice. Prayer enables the pastor to be a calm presence when everyone else may be too involved, too anxious, too busy to pay attention. The calm and prayerful presence of the pastor is often the most needed encouragement for the people.

Spiritual guidance of the whole faith community is important because the congregation is the context in which spiritual growth can take place. Corporate guidance may serve as a catalyst for that growth. Every congregation has its own distinct personality. The pastor needs to have a sense of that uniqueness and to see his or her primary task as dealing with the spirit of the congregation. One may greatly help particular persons but fail to effect change in the congregation. The church, as a living entity, may continue its poor treatment of people or fail to minister.

THE PRACTICE OF SPIRITUAL DIRECTION

The purpose of spiritual direction is to assist persons in the process of discerning God's presence in their lives. In Christian history, we find some particularly helpful writings on the practice of spiritual direction dating from the fourth century. The formal practice of spiritual direction developed as people left the towns to go into the desert, seeking the guidance of persons who had become hermits. The desert offered a place to develop a life centered in God away from the lures of civilization and the compromises of a church that had accommodated itself to being the official church of the Roman Empire.

For many centuries, spiritual direction was a practice within the cloistered communities of religious orders. Because both Protestants and Roman Catholics are rediscovering the importance of spiritual direction for nurturing Christian life in the world, the early writings on spiritual direction offer insight into the basic patterns of interaction. Spiritual guidance is an outgrowth of the ancient tradition of spiritual direction, an adaptation of spiritual direction in less formal settings.

The Graduate Program in the Art of Spiritual Direction at San Francisco Theological Seminary defines spiritual direction this way: "A covenant friendship between Christians in which one assists the other in the discernment of God's presence and the contemplative living out of God's call." The term *covenant friendship* implies the importance of relationship as the core of the Christian life. We all need help from others in order to listen and respond to God. Unaided, we often misunderstand and misinterpret our deepest experiences. Caught up in the whirl of events, we forget God or push the spiritual pilgrimage into the recesses of our lives. That fact emphasizes the importance of understanding spiritual direction as a relationship, a "covenant friendship" between two Christians. Because spiritual direction goes to the heart of our faith questions, it requires a spiritual friend who shares our basic faith.

Spiritual direction is a relationship characterized by covenant because of its careful structure. One of the two parties seeks out the other for help and remains in the position of directee. The helping party is the director. Their mutual agreement involves how often they meet, where they meet, and other aspects of the relationship. Yet the two are also friends who share their faith and their spiritual pilgrimages with each other. The spiritual director does not sit passively while the other person pours out her or his heart but enters into the relationship without fear of being known.

The basis of the relationship between the director and the directee is one of complete trust. The directee must be willing to consider seriously the advice given even when it may be hard to hear. Most of us have few relationships based on the kind of trust that enables us to hear the full, and sometimes painful, truth about ourselves. Often to maintain relationships, we withhold information or tell only part of the story. Even between the best of friends, real trust is rare; we reveal only part of who we are.

Margaret Guenther, in a beautiful book on the subject of spiritual direction, describes the difficulty of establishing trust: "There is the shame of the recovering addict, the lingering sense of uncleanness that haunts the incest survivor, the painful memory of an abortion, the anguish of broken relationships that can never be restored, the burden of trespasses long ago forgotten by all save the trespasser."[1] Because the content of spiritual direction requires complete honesty from the one seeking direction, there can be no holding back of information in any area of life. The directee must trust completely the one who will serve as director if disclosure is to occur without fear.

Building trust may take months, especially if a professional has betrayed the directee's trust in the past. In this relationship, the one giving direction must avoid jumping to conclusions, making judgmental statements, becoming condescending, critical, or abusive of the relationship. Most directees will proceed, bit by bit, to share pieces of their lives. They anxiously await their reception before sharing more. Even then, what they say and what they do not say carry equal weight, and the director must be aware of the significance of nonverbal communication. Sometimes people will say more without words through their tone of voice, posture, or movement.

Our highly individualistic society fosters desperate loneliness. People often hold their deepest fears, their fondest hopes, and their most frightening temptations inside—never revealing their extreme inner pain or its source. Yet many people are looking for someone who will listen with compassion. Their friends, neighbors, or other church members may not offer an understanding ear. The relationship of director and directee becomes sacred because of the deeply personal nature of the material.

The director invites the directee to attend to the events of his or her life closely as clues or signs of God's activity and helps that person probe the meaning of his or her experiences, interpreting the events in the light of faith in God. The process discourages haste as one attempts to ascertain God's presence in life events. Even a good decision made in haste can be destructive. The director helps the directee sort carefully through his or her experience with patience and care to come to decisions about what to do. We call this process discernment, a long-term process of thoughtful discovery of God's intentions in daily life.

The other desired conclusion of spiritual direction is the contemplative living out of God's call. Spiritual direction has important consequences in the pace and shape of a life. Characteristics of persons offering spiritual direction would include their being more reflective, more patient with self and with God, more accepting of certain weaknesses in self and others, and more willing to make hard decisions based on faith. Through this care and acceptance, the life of the directee can become more gentle, loving, and trusting, and less critical, impatient, and angry. If spiritual direction does not move the directee in such ways, then reassessment of the relationship is needed. Perhaps the spiritual director is not a good match for the directee, or something is blocking the progress of the relationship. Sometimes changing directors will help; other times the problem rests within the person who, at some level of the subconscious, may resist any probing of a personal issue.

Our society has chosen unconsciously to place a high value upon personal freedom at the expense of community. Personally we find ourselves very free, especially in the urban centers. We do not have to follow our parents' model or be accountable to anyone else. We honor our freedom as a cherished part of American culture. The down side of this privatization of life is that we often have no natural community to which we belong.

The terrible loneliness of many persons within Western culture stems from a combination of factors: urban stress, suburban flight, the decline of the extended family, and other factors. Spiritual direction represents a needed kind of friendship. People are realizing their need to tell the truth about themselves and their relationship with God, as well as their need to enhance their faith to grow in their relationship with God. Loneliness coincides with the increased interest in spiritual direction.

An important value of the ecumenical tradition is that most Protestants have, of necessity, been able to choose Roman Catholics as their spiritual directors. These Catholics, already trained in ancient traditional practices, have wisdom far beyond their own particular spiritual tradition. Although spiritual direction is still a new discipline among Protestants, more Protestant directors are receiving training in spiritual direction.

SPIRITUAL DIRECTION AND PASTORAL COUNSELING

Spiritual direction and counseling share many characteristics. The structure of both personal relationships requires certain promises and expectations of each party. Both spiritual direction and counseling constitute formal helping relationships. Both disciplines require mutual trust. The person seeking help must trust the helper with personal matters that go to the core of his or her being. The one doing the helping must respect and trust the one seeking help. This trust includes confidence that the directee is capable of making wise decisions.

Both disciplines involve talking about the life experience of the person who has come for help. Both often begin with questions: How do I deal with this situation? Where do I go from here? What should I do next? Both also look toward changed attitudes in the life of the person coming for help. No responsible counselor or spiritual director would agree to work with anyone without some expectation of the possibility of change and growth in the other. To enter into any relationship without such an expectation would be dishonest. For Christians, such optimism lies at the very heart of our faith; we believe that with God nothing is impossible.

At the same time, both counseling and spiritual direction are careful not to impose change: Both seek free decisions and appropriate growth. Both counseling and spiritual direction involve limits; the one offering help realizes that it may be necessary to refer the person to another skilled professional.

Despite these important similarities, important differences

may surface. Counseling usually begins with a personal problem, a situation that becomes the focus of the discussion. The problem may be a cause of pain and frustration, an issue that may interfere with life goals or get in the way of healthy relationships.

Persons enter spiritual direction with a different motive. The directee does not seek help with a particular problem, and the relationship is not established to deal with a current situation. In spiritual direction, the directee's primary concern is to deepen his or her relationship with God. The whole focus is upon God's presence in that person's life. In spiritual direction, the Holy Spirit consciously becomes a third party.

At times spiritual direction and counseling look alike: The same material may surface in both kinds of sessions. Whatever the person seeking help considers important must be accepted as appropriate material—personal relationships, interior temptations, work struggles, marital problems, and ethical issues. Sometimes both pastoral counseling and spiritual direction will uncover issues that have remained buried.

However, spiritual direction approaches that same material with a different focus. The spiritual director watches for evidence of the Spirit's movement in the life of the directee. The director looks for signs of spiritual growth in the person, for clues about the way the material events of life become blocks to faith or avenues for new depth. The questions the director raises will not focus on finding solutions to the problems but on the ways in which the problems offer potential sources for spiritual maturity, for self-discovery, for trust in God, and for possible transformation.

Spiritual direction requires a nondomineering approach and attitude on the part of the director. The director must maintain a clear perspective on his or her ability to be of help.

Every director needs to resist the temptation to "fix" the directee. The director is not in charge of the other person's life. The director simply points the directee in the right direction: toward God. God is the real director of souls.

The most important ingredient in spiritual direction is faith on the part of both the directee and director. The one seeking direction gives the director the great gift of trust and openness. The director responds to this gift with gentleness and loving attention. Both must trust that God is involved in whatever transpires. Such faith keeps both motivated in the search for proper discernment. Such faith grounds all that takes place in a context of God's loving concern. That grounding asserts that God can be counted upon to enter into the life of the one seeking direction—in fact, that God is already present.

The director helps the other person by listening intently to God's journey in that person's life. The biographical material is not the primary focus. Directors return again and again to the subject of what God is about in the life of the directee. The director's questions may sound like these: What signs of grace are operating in your life? How does this situation affect the way you pray? Where do you see signs of God's presence in your life experiences? What faith issues seem most pressing?

The central goal of all spiritual direction is discernment. The director is "simultaneously a learner and a teacher of discernment."[2] Discernment is the difficult process of learning to sift through one's life experiences in order to discover what God is about, to learn to distinguish those impulses that come from God from among a number of competing claims. The goal is to avoid mistaking one's own urges for the will of God. To the end that the directee may be helped to discern God's voice, the director will listen intently and prayerfully, sharing his or her perceptions honestly.

If, for example, the director notices a danger in the directee's life, the director will speak candidly about this observation. The director will temper candor with gentleness and respect for the other person's integrity. Every director must approach his or her task with proper humility, a willingness to recognize that no single person has all the answers and the knowledge that God is a great mystery, even beyond the grasp of the wisest and saintly of souls.

How does one discern what is going on in the soul of another person? Perhaps the best single clue is the growth in that person of the Spirit's gifts: love, joy, peace, patience, kindness, fidelity, gentleness, and self-control. (See Galatians 5:22.) If these qualities are developing in the person's life, then that person's relationship to God is growing. However, it should be noted that persons can misunderstand and misinterpret these gifts. Mindless enthusiasm can masquerade as joy; boredom may resemble patience; and depression can look like peace.

God's mystery operates in the life of both director and directee. Trusting in God, who is at work before our awareness, is basic for all discernment. Such trust keeps us from believing that what we do is ultimately essential. God is present even when we misread clues or give unwise advice. Faith in God's graciousness in the life of the other person is the basis of the relationship; we dare to engage in spiritual direction because we know the Holy Spirit's power and presence accompany us.

By paying attention to the events of a person's life and looking for the connections among various threads of that life, we recognize God at work. The events are not random; they form a pattern pointing to God's activity. To become aware requires our attention; to know something is to recognize it as coming from its true source; to be open is to name God's involvement.

A MODEL OF SPIRITUAL DIRECTION

Although personalities and styles may differ, some common characteristics of a session of spiritual direction include the following:

1. *Greeting.* A greeting begins every direction session. The director welcomes the other person into the space prepared, offers a seat, expresses delight in the presence of the other, and is genuinely hospitable. Preoccupation or over-extension of self prevents a director's offering such hospitality.

2. *Prayer.* Prayer in some form is the beginning of all direction. It may be a form of silent centering prayer that marks this time as different from what has gone before. Quietness enables the readiness of both parties to receive the Spirit's leading. The prayer time may involve lighting a candle to suggest holy space and time. It also may involve spoken prayer to invoke the Holy Spirit's presence and the openness of the participants to that presence.

3. *Questions.* A question or two of the directee may begin the time together as the director attempts to discover what is happening, how a motive for change has actually worked, what has happened to a resolution, or what has blocked the development of some intended course of action. These questions should be asked with great care to respect the pace the directee wishes to maintain.

4. *Major content.* The bulk of every session rests with the directee. The director encourages the directee to face things that may be unpleasant, assists the directee in making honest assessment of his or her own life, helps the person see strengths and weaknesses in a situation, and affirms the directee's empowerment to claim God's freely extended

love. The director may ask about dreams or explore life situations. The director may ask about journal writings and encourage the directee to share something written. The director probes for the sole purpose of helping the directee delve into deeper understanding of his or her own relationship with God.

5. *Space for the work of the Spirit.* No one can determine the content of a direction session ahead of time. Content will develop from the directee's material. Often what takes place may surprise both director and directee. We cannot plan for or manipulate the work of the Holy Spirit.

6. *Suggestions.* The director may suggest particular avenues for the directee's pursuit before the next session, such as a prayer form, dialogue with a specific passage of scripture, giving particular attention to the journal, or some other practice. Burdening the directee with too many expectations should be avoided.

7. *Closing.* The session will end with spoken prayer, perhaps by the director only or by both the director and the directee.

Most direction sessions will follow the above format or a similar one.

NOT EVERY PASTOR SHOULD BE A SPIRITUAL DIRECTOR, although every pastor would probably benefit from having a spiritual director. The pastor cannot possibly have time for this kind of intensive personal work any more than she or he does for individual pastoral counseling. The pastor may encourage one or more members of the congregation who have real gifts for leadership to receive training as spiritual directors. These trained lay spiritual directors could focus upon a ministry of one-on-one spiritual direction as part of the church's ministry.

SPIRITUAL GUIDANCE AND CONGREGATIONAL LIFE

The pastor as spiritual guide for the congregation can make a difference in the nature of the congregation. This difference occurs through the way the pastor attends to the spiritual needs of the congregation: its wounds and its signs of health. Change will happen when the pastor sees his or her major responsibility not as successfully maintaining the institution but as successfully leading the people into a deeper relationship with God. Pastoral work is soul work, whether practiced with individuals or with groups, and every aspect of pastoral activity should serve the overall aim of the spiritual growth of the congregation.

The pattern found in spiritual direction sessions can shape components of every major pastoral activity. First, *greeting:* The pastor in relationship to the congregation offers hospitality, inviting people into the sacred space and time that serve as parameters of congregational life. Second, *prayer:* The pastor prays for the people and for the congregation as a whole. Third, *listening:* The pastor attends to the congregation's life, paying careful attention to signs of spiritual health or disease and to movements of the Holy Spirit. Fourth, *questions:* The pastor probes with gentle questions to discern what God is about among this particular group of people. Fifth, *encouragement:* The pastor is receptive to what the people say and do and encourages them in their ventures of faithfulness. Sixth, *suggestions:* The pastor offers suggestions to the people individually and corporately, only after having gone through the other five steps.

The traditional work of ministry takes on a different perspective when seen through the lens of spiritual guidance. Serving the single purpose of the growth of souls transforms pastoral activity. Through spiritual guidance, pastoral work takes on a different character. Those engaged in pastoral ministry may find new meaning and purpose. As persons attend to the prodding of God's spirit in the congregation, pastoral life will be transformed.

CHAPTER FOUR

The Care of Souls as Spiritual Guidance

PASTORAL CARE has undergone great changes since the turn of the century. Prior to the twentieth century, prayer, scripture, and concern for the faith and its expression in the life of the parishioner shaped pastoral care. Pastors catechized and questioned; they examined and gave advice, often using scripture to reinforce the power of their words. Most of the time they engaged in these activities while visiting in people's homes. Pastors saw their responsibility before God as that of ensuring the spiritual growth of those entrusted to their care. They tried to apply their understanding of the scriptures to the lives of the people for whom they felt accountable before God.

Sometimes pastors responded to complex human dilemmas with rigidity and legalism. They often sought to correct people by moralizing, scolding, or threatening with divine punishment; thereby doing serious emotional and psychological damage. Other pastors felt it their duty to correct wrongdoing by criticizing actions and in the process caused long-term harm to people by adding a burden of unredeemed guilt to their load. Today their direct manner of pastoral care seems overly authoritarian, but much of the time they did more than give advice or correction. They also tenderly listened to the concerns and problems of the people and prayed with and for them. The letters of spiritual guidance and counsel left by pastors from earlier centuries evidence their compassionate concern for their people. This sample from a letter by John Wesley to Mary Bishop demonstrates sensitive pastoral care:

> I think it would not be best for you to go out less you ever did. Suppose you have more faith and more love (as I would fain think you have), you certainly ought to go out more. Otherwise your faith will insensibly die away. It is *by works* only that it can be *made perfect*. And the more the love of solitude is indulged the more it will increase.[1]

Wesley's wisdom about the importance of staying in touch with other people and of avoiding what he called the temptation to solitude is not an isolated instance. Many premodern pastors had deep and sensitive understanding of those who sought them out for guidance. They often referred to pastoral care as the "care of souls" because that term emphasized the spiritual condition of the persons involved. To care for another's soul involved a different type of care than that of mind and body. Because knowledge of the human soul comes only through relationship to God, care for souls implied deliberate care for the way people related to God by paying attention to their spiritual selves.

This premodern method of pastoral care displayed some serious limitations. Pastors were not equipped with an adequate understanding of the human psyche; many were unable to respond to situations that called for more than concern, common sense, and prayer. Because pastors did not understand the human mind in any systematic way, they could make serious mistakes in what they observed, treating an illness or an emotional wound as a sin, for example.

Parishioners, overly anxious to appear at their best before the pastor, would hide or block out embarrassing or shameful problems, many unwilling to reveal their deepest secrets to the pastor. Even those pastors with great natural understanding could not respond in depth because they did not know all the facts. The very power of pastors served to distance them from their people, protected by silence from information about parishioners' everyday lives.

INFLUENCE OF PSYCHOLOGY

The gifts of modern psychology to pastoral care have greatly affected the way pastors function. The contributions of Freud, Adler, Jung, and other pioneers in psychology began to make their way into American higher education early in the twentieth century. In the period between World War I and World War II, pastoral psychologists began to use the resources of these giants. Knowing more about the human psyche enabled the growth and development of pastoral care and made it possible for pastors to listen more carefully and more sympathetically than without such knowledge. Pastors educated in psychology pick up signs of illness or clues that point to deeper problems more quickly. Many pastors have become highly skilled as counselors. Clergy properly trained in the tools of psychology have helped many people greatly. The ability of trained pastors to listen effectively to the worst that people can tell about their secret sins without fear of condemnation is but one significant benefit of these tools.

One drawback to the development of pastoral counseling skills is that psychology has generally replaced theology in shaping pastoral care; the language of psychology has become the language of pastoral care. We live in an era in which we view everything and everyone from a psychological perspective. In the process of becoming more psychological, we have diminished the spiritual perspective. Pastors, concerned about being good, nonjudgmental listeners and worried about intruding into the lives of others, frequently have neglected prayer as a major tool for pastoral care. Hesitating to venture an opinion about the theological nature of the parishioner's situation has been seen as healthy. Pastors take care to hear people before invading their lives or seeking to control them with the power of God. Pastors have come to realize that people do not necessarily turn to them in order to be "fixed," and they certainly do not want the pastor to take over their lives.

The model for pastoral care has become that of helping each person see the strengths within himself or herself and to move toward discovery of inner resources. The assumption behind this nondirective practice is that persons have inner truth about themselves deep within that provides guidance and strength if encouraged. Instead of imposing one's own opinions upon the other person, the pastoral role has become that of a catalyst to assist others in the process of becoming healthy. These insights of the pastoral care model have encouraged many people to see themselves in new ways; to break negative patterns of thought and behavior; and to grow in self-esteem, faith, and practice. Failure to recognize the importance of modern psychology to pastoral care is a grave mistake. We cannot go backward and pretend that we can dispense with the insights that psychology has taught us.

Yet people who turn to a pastor for counseling often expect a more theological and explicitly religious experience than is possible from the nondirective response. Individuals may not know how to articulate what they seek, but nondirective therapy techniques are insufficient to produce desired change in the one seeking help. Pastors who employ nondirective therapy techniques exclusively may have many counselees who come away from a visit feeling vaguely uneasy. They wish the pastor had talked about God, had prayed, had made some suggestions, had even offered forgiveness in the name of God for some sin they have confessed.

Had they wanted good psychological counseling, these parishioners could have gone to a counseling center or to a psychiatrist. They wanted something different, whether or not they could name what they sought. At some level, they were looking for some clue about eternal matters, and the psychologist did not provide it. They may have been looking for healing from some emotional scar or painful memory that they had borne for too many years. They may have desired release from guilt, from grief over paths not taken and bad choices made. They surely wanted the pastor to nourish their souls. Thus they were disappointed in their search even if they received excellent professional counseling. Persons often come to pastoral counseling situations expecting God to be part of the encounter. If the pastor says nothing about God or does not offer to pray, the counselees may experience frustration, a sense of something missing, a feeling of incompleteness.

The pastoral task is primarily that of caring for people's souls so that they discover their own healing as a gift from God. To care for souls, pastors need to be well grounded in the faith and, at the same time, have some appreciation for the human mind and the ways it can express sickness and health in issues such as transference and projection. Few pastors understand the human psyche well enough to become professional counselors; they will always be amateurs in this arena. Unless pastors know and appreciate their own limitations, they may do damage by attempting to go beyond their ability.

Pastors' training encompasses the Christian faith, its symbols and its language. Among professionals, their training is unique at this point. And with this training, pastors can provide what no one else can: They can help people discover ultimate meaning in the midst of life situations. Such soul care is a matter of releasing others into God's presence. The care of souls as a model for ministry means paying close attention to what God is doing in a given life. It requires an attitude of quiet reflection and careful attentiveness to each person but also an attitude of receptiveness to God cultivated by the practice of prayer. The pastor who cares for the souls of the people works in faith, affirming God's loving involvement in their lives. Only with this faith and affirmation can the pastor dare to assist parishioners in the process of their spiritual growth.

THE FIVE STEPS OF SPIRITUAL GUIDANCE

Every pastor would do well to consider the model of spiritual guidance for the pastoral care of individuals and families. Just as spiritual guidance is a process of paying prayerful attention to the presence and action of God in a situation, so pastoral care uses that same skill to deal with the problems of the people. In a one-on-one relationship, the spiritual guide's responsibilities are these:

1. to listen carefully to what people say about themselves and their spiritual lives,

2. to encourage their desire (expressed or hinted at) to recognize and respond to God's presence in their lives,

3. to suggest the practice of certain disciplines that will enable spiritual growth and open them to the Holy Spirit's presence,

4. to challenge them to examine their lives honestly in the light of God's forgiving love, and

5. to pray with and for them.

Each of these five steps in classic spiritual guidance is an appropriate part of the pastoral care process.

1 *Listening carefully*, paying attention to what is said, and watching for clues in both words and acts are the roots of pastoral care. At this point, care of souls, spiritual guidance, and good pastoral counseling come together with a common goal. Each of these somewhat different disciplines involves paying close attention to the other person. Real listening is a learned art. Often what we identify as listening usually is our waiting to change the subject, give advice, or otherwise turn the focus away from the person. Genuine care for others expresses itself in our willingness to hear them, to be fully present for them, to notice all the clues they give—words spoken, words not spoken, discomfort expressed in body language or tone of voice. By paying attention we tell others that we value them, that they deserve our attention. Without attention, we can easily draw the wrong conclusions, jump to incorrect assumptions, fail the counselees by treating them as if they were in the way or keeping us from more important tasks. To really listen implies that we take persons seriously, that we value their presence, that we treat them as eternally important.

Flora Slosson Wuellner in her book *Feed My Shepherds* has posed some excellent questions for pastors to ask themselves:

- Am I able to listen quietly without quick simplistic answers, diagnosis, and advice?

- Am I able to discern and assist in the decision as to whether the problem or wounding is beyond my skills and requires therapeutic professional attention?…

- Am I able to affirm and encourage the other in self-worth, dignity, and essential empowerment?…

- Can I encourage the other to trust his or her own instincts and to allow the other to express and define the feelings present?

- Am I able to discern and clarify practical helps?...

- Am I able to keep from pushing or rushing the other to conclusions, healing, and closure? Do I have a strong inner agenda for this person?

- Am I aware of my own inner self so that I am not drained by the other? Am I internalizing the darkness or pain of the other within my own body, my own space? Am I aware of the need of appropriate bodily and emotional boundaries between myself and the other?...

- Am I able to pray for and with this person in a way that does not concentrate solely upon the problem but releases the whole person into Christ's healing hands?[2]

Simply asking these questions can be an excellent tool for discernment of one's own gifts and weaknesses as a listener. The self-discovery can help any of us seek the training to hone our skills. The goal is to be good listeners.

2 *Encouragement* means caring for another person not as part of a process, not as a hindrance, not as a case study for analysis, not as something broken that needs fixing; but as a person who has a right to his or her own feelings and a right to express those feelings openly without fear of scolding, criticism, or correction. Encouraging other persons to express feelings openly requires confidence in the relationship on the part of both pastor and parishioner. Parishioners gradually learn to trust that the pastor is not trying to change them, abuse them, or control them. Then and only then can the pastor make any suggestions about ways the counselees might

open themselves to God. A relationship of trust engenders the confidence necessary to speak their minds and to be able to respond with trust.

Many people do not believe they matter; they have learned to think too little of themselves. This low self-opinion has come from parents, teachers, and other sources. They do not trust their own ideas or value their own thoughts. This low self-opinion may be their response to pastoral urgings to be humble. Yet humility differs from having a low opinion of self. Instead of growing out of a sense of personal unworthiness, healthy humility stems from a person's belief that he or she is valued and has God-given worth. Humility is acceptance of our worth and thus our ability to put aside our needs to meet the needs of another. Our belief in our own worth enables us to give ourselves to others. Because of the confusion between genuine humility as a virtue and low self-opinion as a problem, pastors must understand the need for all people to value themselves as God's creatures. Such self-valuing serves as an expression of gratitude to God.

We reinforce self-worth by holding up achievements to be celebrated. Everyone has some accomplishments. We encourage persons when we help them review their lives. Life review can provide an occasion for the pastor gently to guide the parishioner to see his or her life in the perspective of God's grace by celebrating joys and grieving sorrows.

3 *Assisting persons to grow spiritually* means that pastors move beyond listening and encouraging to making suggestions about how persons may discern God. Note an important difference between the work of a pastor and that of other psychological professionals: The pastor enters into the counseling process with theological understandings and is able

to offer clues to the person in a careful and thoughtful way. This step can take place only when the pastor has earned the full confidence of the person. The parishioner trusts that the pastor's suggestions are for his or her own good and are motivated by the pastor's genuine interest in him or her. Also, the counselee must be able to trust that the pastor's advice comes from his or her own Christian faith and experience. Parishioners will trust their pastor if they believe they can accept or reject the advice in freedom without harming the relationship or hurting the pastor's feelings.

Each of these qualities must be present if the pastor's suggestions are to be received and accepted. The advice may include suggestions about rest, prayer, self-care; or it may include suggestions about referral to another professional.

The pastor's special task is that of assisting others in the fine art of attending to God. Assisting the parishioner to grow will involve guidance in discernment. Discernment is the delicate process of paying attention to one's own life in such a way as to gain clarity about God's action. The person considers clues that may suggest the movement of the Holy Spirit. Such clues include an examination of the consequences of a particular action. The pastor may be the only one in a position to help the counselee ask the painful questions of what a particular act may produce for the person and that person's wider family. Discernment also includes helping the person pay attention to his or her own feelings: Does reflecting about a proposed action bring a sense of peace and relief? Does it cause agitation, anxiety, or second thoughts? The pastor may suggest particular forms of attentive behavior such as meditation, reflective reading of scripture, or silent prayer. Such suggestions are important forms of pastoral care. The pastor may

need to teach one or more spiritual practices as aids to attentiveness in discerning the Holy Spirit's movement in persons'
lives. Part of what the pastor needs to bring to a given pastoral
care situation is skill in the art of discernment and the ability
to teach discernment.

Another important skill for all pastors is the art of referral.
This art frees pastors from attempting to treat cases for which
they have no training or preparation. Knowing when to refer
requires some understanding of the nature of the human psyche. The pastor must be able to tell when the parishioner is out
of touch with reality, when he or she is absorbed in fantasy, or
when transference has caused confusion about boundaries.
Every pastor must pay close attention to his or her limits, recognizing when feelings of being overwhelmed by another person should suggest referral.

4 *Challenging* is the next step in pastoral care. Such challenges can take place only when the pastor has earned
the right to be taken seriously by the other person. A
special gift is given when any person trusts another enough to
take seriously what is said, especially when it may be hard to
hear. Most people can hear what they want to hear or what
they expect to hear, but the real gift of trust is to be able to hear
what is said when it is either too good to believe or can be
interpreted as a criticism of the person. Some parishioners
need to hear the hard truth about their abuse of some sub-
stance, for example. Many areas of life cry out for the speaking
of unpleasant truth. Healing can begin only when we have
spoken the truth, when we have heard the truth about ourselves uttered tenderly and with understanding. We all need
help to discover destructive patterns in our lives: overeating,
compulsive overwork, or any other area of life that has gotten

out of balance. To pretend that all is well is dishonest, and pastoral relationships build on truth.

Many pastors have a need to be liked and accepted by others. This need may lead them to be very attentive, but it also may interfere with their ability to speak the truth in love. Yet hard truth may make the difference between a life that turns around and a life that self-destructs. Telling the truth to another person includes accepting responsibility for the way that truth is both conveyed and received. In telling the truth, pastors have to exercise care so the counselee does not perceive it as interference or an authoritarian effort to dominate. To the extent that pastoral advice arises from genuine care for the other person, it is unlikely to be so perceived.

Before any pastor challenges a parishioner, the pastor needs to ask, What is my motive for speaking? Do I want to speak out of a genuine desire to help, or is it a desire to be in charge? The same questions should be asked about avoidance of truth: Have I refrained from speaking about the parishioner's behavior patterns out of a respect for the other person or out of a fear of rejection? Do I care more about the growth of this parishioner or my own appreciation? These questions cannot be ignored. Pastors must pay careful attention to their own fears and to their own desires for power. Both fear and power can destroy a pastoral relationship.

The best way to assist others in self-discovery lies in leading them to discover the truth about themselves. Some people have developed elaborate systems of self-deceit, living in a fantasy world of their own making. A pastor in a counseling relationship can help them peel away the lies and half-truths, layer by layer. As persons expose each layer of untruth, they come closer to knowing their real selves. Honesty leads to self-disclosure; this process, while slow and painful, leads to growth. Yet the pastor must avoid hurrying the process of growth. Over-eagerness to help the other person progress may indicate mistrust of the Holy Spirit's work in the life of the other person. No one has the right to manage another's life. Efforts to dominate refuse the respect due the other person. Respect is a necessary factor in all healthy human relationships. Because we believe that God is already present in the lives of those who come for help, pastors can offer the gift of confidence to those who seek them out. We can dare to sit with, care for, and pray for the troubled because we believe they are loved by the gracious God who wills their health and wholeness.

5 *Prayer with and for the other* is an integral part of the relationship between the pastor and parishioner. When a parishioner asks for prayer, the pastor must take this request seriously. To agree to pray for another makes one accountable to God. Of course, the pastor also will offer unsolicited prayer. Sometimes parishioners may not want the pastor to pray, but those moments will be rare. Most of the time, they will welcome prayer. They may have hoped secretly that the pastor would pray but were embarrassed to ask or feared their desire for prayer would make the pastor uncomfortable. When the pastor offers to pray, most people will be relieved and grateful. They are dealing with their spiritual leader, not a secular professional. The offer of prayer may not be what that person most needs, but it is certainly far better to err on the side of such an offer than to ignore a crying need for prayer and to leave the parishioner feeling spiritually bereft.

THE RESULTS OF THIS APPROACH

By using a model of spiritual guidance in pastoral care, the pastor assists individuals in noticing God's action in their lives, in paying attention to signs of God's grace in life's ordinary events, and in responding to God's invitation to be about the work of love and justice in their lives. Through this process, pastors can assist people who come to them develop a clearer understanding of themselves and of their deepest needs and problems. Leadership in the church, or for that matter, in most organizations is not so much knowing the right information and dispensing it to the ignorant as it is learning to develop a sense of presence. In the church, the presence is of God. Spiritual guidance is the intentional development of a holy presence in the person of the leader, and through that leader, in the whole congregation.

This presence does not come automatically. Unless pastors deliberately bring God into conversations, people may talk about everything else. Unless the pastor suggests prayer, the people may not know how to ask for it. Unless the pastor raises questions about the connection between faith and the personal issues in daily life, parishioners may not make that connection.

Above all, pastoral care is care for people's spiritual lives. Pastoral care dares to name persons' situations in specifically religious language and to offer specifically religious opportunities for growth. God is a party to every form of ministry, including pastoral care.

Sometimes a pastor can make the connection between pastoral care and spirituality through physical location: Counseling people in the church sanctuary instead of in the pastor's office is one possibility. To be surrounded by the symbols of the faith is to be reminded of God's grace, to have hope that no matter how difficult or hopeless one feels at a given moment of time, the everlasting arms are present to comfort and sustain. When the pastor counsels in a study or office, pictures on the walls need to be chosen carefully so they reflect the fact that this room is part of the church's ministry. A cross or a picture of Jesus could make a real difference in assisting persons to claim the resources of faith for themselves.

Insights of modern psychology may bless every aspect of pastoral work, preventing clergy from jumping to the wrong conclusions and encouraging them to be aware of unhealthy signs of dependence, as well as the possible need for referral. But the pastor is more than a professional counselor; the pastor is a therapist of the soul who specializes in the interior matters of a person's relationship with God and the power of that relationship to bring healing. The pastor brings the potential power of the message of the gospel to the person who is plagued by doubt or guilt. A powerful word of forgiveness, spoken at the right moment in a counseling situation, may be the single most important contribution a pastor can make.

Pastoral care that uses the model of spiritual guidance relies upon the unique insights of Christian faith. The pastor—no matter what the situation, no matter how well-trained in psychology—is first and foremost one whose very presence speaks of the presence of God and whose words can bring new life out of the deadness of people's situations because they speak of the God who cares about people however stained and soiled they may feel they are.

Nearly every Protestant denomination has rediscovered the renewal of the ancient practice of hearing confession of sin and pronouncing words of God's forgiveness. Services of reconciliation, as they are called, have been introduced into the new liturgical materials for pastoral care. This addition to the liturgical materials coincided with Roman Catholic congregations' minimizing the role of priest as confessor and emphasizing the role of the whole congregation in reconciliation. This ironic shift reflects the revolutionary character of contemporary liturgical renewal. Both forms of confession and reconciliation are necessary. Much of the time, the corporate confession of the congregation is sufficient. At times, however, individuals need to speak their own words of confession aloud to another person who will hear them and speak words of assurance to them directly. Until this happens, they carry a sense of unforgiven sin around with them.

The pastor can be the person to whom the wounded, burdened, and troubled may turn in the hope of finding release from that which weighs them down. The pastor possesses the power to bring healing through the forgiving words that are part of the vocabulary of ministry. Acting in the name of Jesus, the pastor can say what people most desperately want and need to hear. The pastor can hear their worst, look them in the eye, and pronounce the blessed words of assurance and God's gracious pardon—perhaps even marking them with the sign of the cross. When this happens, the pastor is privileged to watch the shedding of old burdens and the birthing of new and freer selves.

The pastor offers the gifts of spiritual guidance to those who seek him or her, and in the process realizes that these gifts are not only welcomed but carry power for the transformation of persons and situations. This model of pastoral care helps people discover the availability of God's power to heal them and their relationships. Confession and forgiveness are powerful aids in the healing of guilt; they are tools that are unique to the work of the pastor.

CHAPTER FIVE

Worship as Spiritual Guidance

WORSHIP IS CENTRAL to every congregation's life; it both expresses and shapes congregational life. Worship is the primary activity for which the whole congregation gathers, the major reason for the congregation's existence, and the most important activity in which humans engage.

Worship is also the principal avenue for the nurture and maintenance of congregational spiritual life. What happens in worship greatly impacts the quality of people's faith and commitment. The corporate worship experience also will influence the way new people perceive a church and their decision either to enter its life or to look elsewhere.

A pastor seeking to nurture the congregation as a spiritual body has a unique opportunity in the worship service each Sunday when a significant percentage of the membership is present, reasonably expectant, and available for growth. The people have come with their desire for the spiritual food necessary to sustain them for the coming week. One of the miracles of the church is that many people continue to attend in the hope that *this* Sunday's worship may lead them to a new and deeper sense of God's reality, even a sense of the holy mystery of God's presence. They maintain this hope even after having been disappointed many Sundays. These people are present, waiting, responsive, and willing to be led into new depth.

To understand the connection between spirituality and the worship life of the congregation, we need to question the connection between spirituality and the church itself: To what extent does our spirituality depend upon or even relate to the institutional church? The answer may be obvious to pastors who plan and lead worship; but many people, even active church members, find little connection. They may participate in church worship, but many would acknowledge that their real spiritual growth takes place elsewhere—in private settings or in small groups outside the church. To the question "Does church worship nurture your faith?" many sensitive church members would respond unhesitatingly, "No!" They might not express disappointment or anger about this state of affairs because they do not believe that worship's intention is to provide for their personal needs. They may have internalized a sermon on how worship is something we offer to God; they are not expecting worship to meet their needs. They have been told that expecting to have personal needs met in worship is selfish and wrong. As a result, they have arbitrarily separated worship from spiritual development.

RENEWAL OF WORSHIP

Participating in a church forces people to deal with others' needs and expectations. For those seeking purposeful change, the cumbersome processes by which churches make changes never seem to move quickly enough. Because a large number of people have to agree on a common agenda, the church changes more slowly than many would like. Consensus is hard to achieve.

In no area of a church's life is consensus more difficult to achieve than in the worship service. If some push for change too rapidly, others resist with dire threats of withholding funds or quitting. Those resisting enjoy certain styles of hymns, prayers, liturgies; they do not want to change. On the other hand, some people find the typical Protestant worship service boring or incomprehensible. Frequently these people did not grow up in the church. They have no favorite hymns. They neither know nor love scripture, and they find the language of worship quaint at best. Unlike traditionalists, these people make little noise; they may visit and never return. They turn elsewhere for fulfillment of their spiritual needs—perhaps to a New Age group or to a "seeker-friendly" congregation that is eager to meet their needs and willing to adapt the tradition accordingly. Because of the diverse expectations, worship will not please everyone no matter how hard the pastor tries.

Worship will not please everyone despite the best efforts of the pastor and the worship committee. If leaders leave worship the way it has always been, most of the regular attenders will be reasonably content, but newcomers may be put off and not return. If leaders attempt to effect change in worship, criticism may be intense (depending upon the suddenness and degree of change) from the regular attenders, and newcomers may still find the worship antiquated and irrelevant. No wonder many pastors despair. Pastors face no more troubling task than that of putting together a worship experience that meets the diverse expectations of church members and potential members.

Part of the reason for the difficulty lies in the context of our work today. There was a time when worship was taken for granted. Sunday after Sunday, one did what had always been done. Publishers printed hymnals to last for decades, and pastors limited hymn choice to those in the official denominational hymnal. We now live in a time of unprecedented change in worship.

In a post-Vatican II world, everything suddenly became thinkable. Rome had revolutionized itself. The change was not gradual but a dramatic respiriting of the worship life of the Roman Catholic Church. New life was breathed into rituals that had become repetitious, monotonous, and nearly meaningless to most worshipers. Ever since the Vatican Council II, Protestants have had to reexamine themselves. We had shaped a good deal of who we were and what we did or did not do in worship in reaction to Rome. If Catholics knelt for prayer, we would not. If they made the sign of the cross, we would not. If they celebrated Communion weekly, we would not. Biblical, historical, or theological rationales were not as important as keeping our tradition separate from that of Rome. Regardless of the teachings of Luther, Calvin, Wesley, or the traditional heritage of the church, Protestants found themselves stuck in a response pattern set against Roman Catholics.

The Vatican Council II (1962–65) changed the direction of the Roman Catholic Church. The sermon received new emphasis as a means of communicating the gospel. Baptism became a public event with lots of water. The people received both the bread and the wine during Communion. The mass was spoken in the particular language of a people rather than in Latin. Rituals of healing were recovered from the ancient life of the church. Times of participation for spoken prayer replaced the prayers spoken only by the priest with his or her back to the people. With little Catholic hymnody suitable for congregational use, the church introduced Protestant hymnody with urgency. The comfortable and comforting images of Catholicism were no longer accurate. The Catholic Church adopted the liturgical agenda of the Protestant Reformation. How were Protestants to respond to this situation? They could no longer consider Rome the enemy nor could they measure their worship by Roman Catholic practice.

The Protestant liturgical reform movement has been much more gradual than the Roman Catholic revolution, but it has been equally pervasive. In recent years, each Protestant denomination has produced a new hymnal with revised and reordered liturgical standards. The use of the new revised common lectionary is encouraged. All congregations have not adopted these changes, but they are common enough to be obvious to anyone who travels around in the church today.

Congregations that formerly observed the Lord's Supper quarterly have moved to a monthly observance. People may gather in circles to receive the elements of Holy Communion. Participatory spoken prayers by the people generally have replaced the pastoral prayer. The sermon is no longer the concluding act of worship, the climax to prepare people for the altar call. Responsive actions such as prayer, confession of faith, offering of gifts, and expression of concerns for the world and for the mission of the church follow the sermon. Banners, the use of liturgical colors, and other visual reminders have enlivened the barren simplicity of Protestant worship space.

These signs of liturgical reform point to the rebirth of the spirituality of worship. Now we pay closer attention to what we do in worship. Yet a difference exists between reforming worship and renewing faith. As Don E. Saliers reminds us in *Worship and Spirituality*, "All of us know that we can have a beautiful text, beautiful musical settings, the most theologically well-informed prayers, and the best of liturgical furnishings and yet still not have faithful liturgy....Reformed rites do not automatically transform individual and communal lives."[1]

Yet petrified worship services that never vary, that never have an element of surprise, that never move the people beyond themselves, and that never challenge assumptions can get in the way of spiritual renewal. Such services block out the Spirit and make it difficult for the people to be open to God's presence. Routine that lacks focus can keep people from paying attention, which is the single most serious hindrance to the spiritual life. Worship either can help overcome this hindrance or contribute to the problem by filling time with utterly predictable material. It can help people focus on what is real, or it can dull their appetite for God by providing routines that unintentionally serve to separate them from God, insulating them from God's movement in their midst.

Worship That Encourages Spiritual Growth

Because worship is more than an intellectual exercise, it can serve as a primary means for spiritual growth. In John E. Burkhart's words, worship is "responding affirmatively—accepting God, opening life to God, and rejoicing in God's transforming reality."[2] Each phrase is important for our spiritual growth.

We accept God as we respond to God's invitation. To worship is to say yes to grace. Worship begins with God, with God's movement toward us—not with our search for God. We begin worship by hearing what God has to say to us. God addresses us through word and spirit, inviting us into relationship. Our prayers, hymns, and offerings are our response to the divine invitation. We praise God because we trust God. Faith precedes all our actions in the sense that faith is the basis for praise. We offer thanks because we have experienced God's goodness toward us. We declare our faith as another form of affirmation. Our acceptance involves our whole being; our response to God includes our thinking, our feelings, our actions in the world. As Burkhart puts it, "To worship God is to affiliate with God's cause. It is to go with, and not against, the grain of grace."[3] As we go with grace, we discover the company of the One who beckons us into the divine mystery of our own lives. We accept God every time we worship, whether we reflect upon that fact or not. Our very presence is a sign of our readiness to trust, our willingness to be moved, our openness to the Spirit's work.

We open our lives to God. The service of worship builds upon our acceptance of God and moves toward forms through which we open ourselves to God's presence. From the music that plays as the service begins, to the times of quiet within the service, a significant function of worship is that of creating space in which people may experience what it means to make space for God. All of us are vulnerable in some way to the touch of God's presence. Openness to God indicates a willingness to be vulnerable to the possibility that God may speak to us; we ready ourselves to attend to God's presence in the symbols and actions of the ritual and wait expectantly for what is going on in our souls as we participate in the service.

Worship's risk and potential are that we can never know when God's touch will happen. At any moment in the service through the music, the prayers, the scripture, the sermon, the sense of community, or the sacraments, people may discover the reality of God's presence.

The most common block to being open to God is assuming the attitude of spectators. A person sitting back in a posture of criticism or approval is uninvolved. Staying removed from the action can isolate a person from the experience of being open to God. Receptivity demands involvement in the action as an active participant. Macrina Wiederkehr says that our

problem is that we have "gotten used to the cheap grace of being uninvolved. We've gotten used to worshiping with hearts
that aren't converted. Worship coming from an unconverted
heart can only be empty ritual."[4] The real need for renewal of
worship is the renewal of hearts, making them receptive to the
movement of God's Spirit.

Our Protestant fear of ritual as empty form may be a subconscious acknowledgment that we feel our emptiness from
within. We know that our hearts are unconverted, and thus we
know that we can turn any formal ritual into a bare form.
Praying familiar prayers can become nothing more than repetition of words if our hearts are not involved. Therefore, we
often demand something new and different every week to
keep us busy and entertained. We want action that requires our
full attention and thus prevents us from having to go deep
within ourselves. Above all, we do not want much silence. The
more action-packed the service of worship, the more enter-
taining it is likely to be. When worship entertains us, we can
avoid exploring the depths of our souls. Whether the service is
pompous and staid or lively and exciting, worship can be a
mask that separates people from God.

The symbols of worship are loaded with potential for
opening us to God. For centuries they have functioned as
means of grace, helping people discover God's grace available
to them. Gazing at the cross is itself a spiritual discipline. Who
can do this without considering the wonder of God's gift in
Christ who died for each of us? Any picture in a stained glass
window can be an avenue toward discovery of the divine as the
worshiper enters into the experience depicted. As we contem-
plate the picture, we can become part of that which it represents. The simple act of opening the Bible in preparation for
the reading of God's Word is a powerful symbol of the signifi-

cance of what is to follow. The open Bible represents the availability of God's Word. When the book is opened, we are prepared to encounter what lies within its pages. The voices of others who gather around us in prayer or song are an inspiring reminder of the Christian community; we are not alone. Every action in the service and every part of the worship setting point to the divine.

We worship in order to be transformed! We come with all that weighs us down: our feelings of loss, our pains, our sense of betrayal, our struggles between faith and doubt. In the time of worship we discover words, actions, or symbols that reach deep within our souls. We leave with a lighter burden, a new sense of identity, more courage for facing a difficult situation, more will to make a difference in the world, more assurance that life has purpose. Such discoveries are the stuff of human transformation.

The sheer delight in the discovery of our own possibility for transformation is a cause for celebration. It is unnecessary to create an artificial mood or to pump people up into feeling good. The stuff of transformation resides in the power of the gospel proclaimed with fidelity to its message and careful application to the lives of those present. The gospel then becomes a major vehicle to helping people find themselves encountered by Jesus Christ's saving presence. That powerful presence is transformative in itself. Worship creates space in people's hearts and souls so the transforming power can reach them.

Even repetitive words, phrases and actions offer the possibility that we may be able to put away our critical stance, forget the difficulty of doing it right, and release self-concern. Repetition may enable us to experience God's power because we get out of the way. We can relax into the familiar and let the Spirit move. Transformation is the miracle of becoming so filled with a sense of God's purpose that we find ourselves un-willing or unable to go back to life as it was. We are new peo-ple, and we have to live differently.

THE ELEMENTS OF WORSHIP

Each element of the worship service can unleash transforming power. For many Protestants, *scripture* is the first and primary element of worship. The reading and preaching of scripture holds a sacramental character that bears the presence of the liv-ing God. To hear a Bible reading, to take its message into our lives, and to grasp its significance in particular moments is to encounter the presence of the living Christ. When we receive the divine Word in faith, when we open our hearts and minds to that Word, then we discover—in moments when we least expect it—that the external Word has entered our hearts and souls. It has become part of us. The words of scripture have become God's personal word to us.

Protestants have insisted that the power of the Word pro-claimed has an efficacy much like the efficacy the medieval church credited to the sacraments. Although bad sermons exist, the real cause of failure of many sermons is the hardened hearts of the hearers. They are not ready to receive the presence of the living Christ being offered to them. Craig Douglas Erickson puts it this way: "Discerning God's wisdom is hard work; it re-quires a radical openness of spirit. Preoccupation with worldly concerns, distractions, even negative feelings about the preacher —these must all be set aside for the sake of a much larger con-cern: hearing God's word spoken through human words."[5]

Despite the resistance of many in the congregation, every sermon presents an opportunity for spiritual guidance of the whole congregation. The pastor may speak in such a way to the issues that burden the people who resist as to make clear how

God loves them—in and through their experiences. The burden and opportunity of every sermon is to become a vehicle that deepens faith and enhances an awareness of God's presence.

For a sermon to accomplish this purpose, the preacher has to bridge the gap between the ancient text and the current situations of congregational members. Biblical correctness in interpretation is only half the preaching task. The second half completes and validates the first: to connect the biblical text with members' lives, their problems and fears, their joys and anticipations so that they grasp the good news of God's grace in a new and fresh way. In the preached word we expose ourselves to the sacred story; we open ourselves to God's presence; and we discover anew its application to our lives.

A second major element of worship is *hymnody*. Hymns also open us to God's presence. Music touches our hearts. As the musical text carries the words, they have great power to move us. We are much more likely to remember the words of hymns than any other element of worship. Hymns are prayers that become part of us because they have the benefit of being poetry set to music. In times of spiritual crisis, a verse of a familiar hymn may sustain us.

Our hymnals are prayer books. We seem to know instinctively that hymn selection has a great deal to do with our souls' formation. What we sing, we remember; what we remember shapes faith. The power of hymns to move us often depends on their familiarity. This is not to say that worship planners should limit hymn selection to everyone's favorites. To do so is to impoverish the soul. However, effective worship planners will keep in mind the power of the familiar. Every service of worship should provide an opportunity to sing something well known, even a sung response. Only the familiar allows people to take their noses out of the book, perhaps close their eyes, and sing with heart as well as mind.

Every hymnal is a potential treasury of spiritual nourishment, sometimes awaiting discovery and appropriation. Hymns are able to express what is most profound about our faith in a way that captures our whole being: mind, heart, feelings, and sometimes even our bodies. The power of music prods us to nod our heads or even to clap in time. Hymns are central to the development of our spirituality. They shape our images of God, our forms of prayer, our sense of the sacred. They carry thoughts for us on the wings of music.

The third element of worship is *prayer*. Public prayer is a means of grace that strengthens, stretches, and prepares believers for private prayer. Without public prayer, private prayers frequently become narrowly self-centered. The prayers of the community broaden those private prayers and remind each one of the needs of people beyond the narrow circle of friends and family members. Private prayer can degenerate into a hasty ritual, or it can atrophy altogether. The discipline of public prayer calls the congregation beyond itself and serves as a check upon individual laziness and forgetfulness. The increasingly popular form of public prayer in which people express concerns aloud encourages each believer to think of prayer as an endeavor in which all participate, not just the pastor. The pastor remains an important leader of prayer, frequently being the only person who knows the pains, sorrows, and joys of the whole congregation. The pastor is in a unique position to speak to God on behalf of everyone.

Corporate silence is the fourth element of worship; silence is another powerful spiritual discipline. In the silence, the presence of others (perhaps the sound of their breathing) reminds us that we are not alone. We take time to attend to God. We need to say no word, and we need to do nothing except wait upon God. The Religious Society of Friends (Quakers) has discovered the power of corporate silence, and many Protestants are making that same discovery. Silence offers a profound experience of community. Most people have too little silence in their daily lives. They acknowledge their need for silence to avoid becoming frantic over life's rushed pace. Many people respond with delight to opportunities for silence in worship when these opportunities are introduced carefully with sufficient explanation that the people know what to expect.

Begin with short periods of silence just before or after the corporate prayer of confession or just after the sermon. Given one minute of silence, which may seem like an eternity to the worship leader, the people can collect their thoughts and offer them to God. At first, a time of silence will likely be greeted with coughs and other signs of restlessness. Be sure to prepare people carefully so they know what is happening. Provide a pattern for use in the silence such as, "Let us now come before God in silent confession," or "Let us reflect on the sermon as it applies to our own lives." Even thirty seconds of silence can be enough at first. Build gradually to a minute.

The *sacraments* are the fifth element of worship. These sacred actions, by repetition, take on new meaning as we grow and change. The same act can have completely new meaning in each new and different situation. As youth, we find the baptism of a baby charming, perhaps humorous; and we understand baptism as a welcome into a new family. As we grow and mature, we add further meanings to this basic understanding: engrafting into Christ, washing with water for new life, being sealed with the mark of Christ, being claimed as Christ's disciple. The faith community enacts God's unmerited grace each time a helpless baby is baptized. God claims that child despite the child's having done nothing to earn that acceptance. God loves that baby even though the infant is unaware of God's love. Each of these meanings is correct. None stands alone.

Each baptism we witness offers an opportunity to reflect on our own baptism. In witnessing the baptism of another, it is possible to declare, "I am baptized." That simple affirmation can reclaim hope for those who may believe themselves so hopelessly wounded that they have lost their right to belong to God. Such a declaration can be a source of strength and courage when feelings of inadequacy and failure overwhelm us. Each of us has been touched by grace, included in the community of Christ's people, and given the company of fellow saints as we pursue our spiritual journey.

A multiplicity of meanings attaches to the Lord's Supper. This sacrament is many things to different people at different times. Some see Holy Communion primarily as a fellowship meal that binds all together. Others confess that in this meal they experience Christ's presence in a real way, a deeper and more profound way. In this meal, the community celebrates the infusion of the sacred into the ordinary as the loaf and the cup become bearers of the holy. The sacrament offers a foretaste of God's future reign when people will gather from the four corners of the earth to sit together at table.

Part of the power behind the sacrament of Holy Communion is that it defies full explanation. Communion remains mysterious. Too often we depend upon rational thought to interpret and explain our faith. The sacrament does not submit to analysis. It remains beyond our capacity to interpret fully. It bears holiness in mystery. We can only point to our own experience of the power we encounter and attempt to explain what we see happening. All theologies of the sacraments are interpretations of experience.

Experience comes first; we take and eat bread, and we know that we have been encountered by the living Christ. We pour or sprinkle water and experience the inclusive love of God in Jesus Christ. Over and over again we know ourselves as the beloved of God. Our basic experience precedes all theories about what happens. Because the mystery of experience is basic and primary, sacraments are the stuff out of which Christian spirituality can grow most easily.

Much of what we do in worship remains at the level of rationality. We hear, we comprehend. We agree or disagree. We learn something new; we are disturbed or excited by an idea that suddenly speaks directly to us. But with all of that, we may remain uninvolved and prevent ourselves from undergoing the fundamental experience of worship: human transformation.

Those who design worship need to keep in mind that transformation is central to worship. It is not enough to design services that flow nicely or have a central theme or move logically from one element to another. Worship needs to offer people opportunities for encounter with the living God. These opportunities may arise in the times of silent reflection upon the meaning of what has been said or done. The repetition of words or actions may enable people's comfort so that they can let go of the need to "get it right," forget to work at concentration, and simply be present.

Worship is a window onto the holy. Its design and structure should open the window by inviting participation in such ways that people forget themselves and discover the power of community as the vehicle for God's grace. When members come to worship, they are receptive to God's transforming power. Their very presence testifies to their readiness to be changed even if they appear to be rigid and frozen. When pastors and leaders plan worship around the basic expectation of God's transformation, parishioners will see God more clearly and will find the bread of life that God offers.

CHAPTER SIX

Teaching as Spiritual Guidance

T EACHING IS a common activity for all pastors. Most pastors teach adult Bible classes; confirmation classes; new-member classes; and perhaps special classes for particular officers, deacons, Sunday school teachers, or others. The teaching ministry is as ancient as scripture. One of the most commonly used titles for Jesus was "rabbi." Every pastor is in part a modern rabbi. The apostle Paul listed the teaching ministry as essential in every list of spiritual gifts. He placed it alongside preaching and healing as one of the three necessary forms of ministry.

The pastoral ministry of teaching remains basic. Christian faith involves certain essential information that requires understanding for faith development. The basis of the Christian faith is a story; we need to know at least parts of the story in order to mature in the Christian life. Christianity is a way of life. Identifying the markers along the way and learning how to respond to them is the task of Christian education. Education is an integral part of the process of developing Christian identity.

THE POWER OF TEACHING

Teachers have more power than they think; all teachers are in a dangerous position because they can abuse their power. They may try to force their own ideas upon their students, treating them as empty vessels waiting to be filled. Then teaching becomes an invasive, violent, or hurtful activity. The teacher's authority over others can give those who teach an unhealthy sense of power. Some teachers relish the authority their students ascribe to them. Resisting the temptation to arrogance and power is difficult; every teacher must struggle against it.

Students often attribute more wisdom to their teachers than is actually present; the teacher may exercise the role as dispenser of knowledge in a way that creates insecurity in the students. Even when the students' assumption about the superior knowledge of the teacher is accurate, that wisdom is at best a mixed blessing. The wiser the teacher appears to be, the less the students may think of themselves.

All too often, going to class results in an experience of lowered self-esteem. Students become painfully aware of their lack of knowledge; they come away with no joy of discovery, no sense of adventure, no appreciation for the experience but with a sense that all they have to offer is their ignorance. Teaching makes them ashamed of themselves, aware of their failings, and conscious of their limitations. All too often, teaching reduces otherwise competent people to a level of infantilism in which they become dependent upon what they perceive to be the teacher's superior wisdom. If they continue their study with that particular teacher, they do so as children at the feet of a parent-teacher whose knowledge assures them that someone has the answers or at least knows how to find the answers. Thus they demean their own ability and knowledge.

The great power inherent in teaching lies behind Jesus'

scathing attack upon teaching, which Matthew records: "The scribes and the Pharisees sit on Moses' seat; therefore, do whatever they teach you and follow it; but do not do as they do, for they do not practice what they teach" (23:2-3). Jesus does not warn his hearers against the teachings of the scribes and Pharisees; he warns them against emulating their actions. The scribes and Pharisees do not practice what they teach; students must make a clear distinction between the content of what is taught and how the teacher models that teaching. Such a distinction is vitally important lest the students follow a bad example. The scribes and Pharisees do not fit the words of their teaching with the character of their lives; they do not live the way they teach.

At its best, behavior would reflect knowledge. The more one learns about Christian faith, the more one's life should express that knowledge. When this correlation does not occur, the learning simply adds to life's incongruity. The student may perceive such learning as irrelevant. Such an experience leads to the attitude that scholarship does not matter or even to an attitude of anti-intellectualism.

To be misled by following the example of someone whose words are true but whose life does not measure up is still possible. To some extent this problem is universal. Matching our lives with Christian ideals is difficult. No one can really ever say to students, "Do as I do." Instead, we point to Christ as the example toward which we all strive. Modesty, integrity, and honesty require us to admit our failures. At the same time, our words and deeds must reflect some continuity, or the words by themselves are empty. The actions of the pastor as teacher must at least point to the truth and value of the teaching.

Jesus goes on to attack those whose teaching adds to the misery of their students: "They tie up heavy burdens, hard to

bear, and lay them on the shoulders of others; but they themselves are unwilling to lift a finger to move them" (Matt. 23:4).
Christian education can become a burden. Some teachers
appear to believe that the more difficult they make the subject,
the better their teaching. Such an attitude makes the teacher
feel good at the expense of the students who feel only the burden of their ignorance.

A good teacher knows how to assist the student to grow
and learn and enjoy the process. A really good teacher is able
to make learning an exciting discovery in which students
involve themselves. The best learning takes place when students
have been inspired to dig more deeply on their own; then
learning becomes a source of their delight. Good teachers challenge their students to do their best and hold high standards
before them. They will expect a great deal from their students
because they believe in the students' ability, but they also will
adjust the level of difficulty to fit the readiness of the students.

TEACHING AS FORMATION

In his classic book on Christian education *The Teaching Ministry
of the Church*, James D. Smart calls for a return to the teaching
purposes of Jesus. He describes three purposes: 1) intimate
proclamation of the gospel from one person to another; 2)
instruction of the disciples in the full truth of the gospel "so
that they might leave behind their old inadequate understanding of God, of themselves, and of all things in their world."[1] A
third purpose captures these first two purposes: "that the disciples might be trained in mind and heart to exercise just such a
ministry as that of Jesus himself."[2] Smart makes it clear that
teaching is a process of making disciples. Those who learn are
in the process of becoming disciples; they are challenged to
respond with their lives to what they have learned.

First, as proclamation, teaching shares some of the character of preaching. Yet teaching differs because of its intimacy and personal nature. Like preaching, Christian teaching centers upon the gospel. Christian teaching will always present the good news of God's grace, whatever the particular subject for the day. This does not mean that all church education has to be theological or even biblical. But whatever the subject, it has to bear the central message of the gospel, which is reconciliation between humanity and God and people with other people.

Second, Christian teaching serves the purpose of forming disciples. Formation relates to the totality of the learners' lives, not simply to their minds. Good Christian teaching seeks to shape disciples who understand who they are, whose they are, and what they believe. These disciples also know how to apply their faith to everyday decisions. Good teaching is a kind of spiritual formation; such teaching is never content simply to increase the amount of information in the heads of the students. The teacher seeks to change lives by offering a new vision for the learners and by assisting the students to see how the gospel empowers them and how God offers them possibilities for new life.

Third, teaching seeks to form more teachers. Every Christian who learns becomes a teacher of others or should be able to do so. Neighbors and friends often call upon Christians to explain and interpret the faith. Every Christian teaches his or her own children and their friends. Christians sometimes engage in the action of teaching a church school class. The goal of forming new teachers lies behind all teaching.

Every educational situation makes us aware of the difference between what is taught and the process of teaching. To teach truth in a way that does not benefit people is to miss the golden opportunity of the teaching moment. The subject may be worthy but the process of teaching and learning be so negative that people carry away bitterness, anger, exhaustion, and a sense of their own inadequacy rather than growth in faith.

Henri J. M. Nouwen identified the heart of teaching religion in these words: "Education is not primarily ministry because of what is taught but because of the nature of the educational process itself."[3] We have thought that because we were teaching about the Bible, for example, we were engaging in Christian education. Nouwen reminds us that when the teaching method violates the content of what is taught, it makes the learning process essentially non-Christian.

All too often persons consider the process of teaching as giving the students knowledge, filling them with correct information and assuming they can use that information later. Of course, knowledge is important. Christian faith requires a certain amount of understanding; otherwise a person becomes susceptible to every idea, good or bad. The ability to discriminate between wise and unwise ideas is the product of careful teaching and good learning. We cannot avoid the content of the faith. But careful teaching is more than imparting important information. Careful teaching enables persons to grow while learning the necessary information.

Christian educators do not direct their teaching toward future benefits exclusively. In Christian education the learner benefits at the time he or she is learning. The blessing of learning takes place during as well as after the educational experience. Good Christian learning is more than preparing for something that will come later; it also offers the learner an opportunity to exercise Christian virtues while learning. The class session can challenge as well as affirm one's abilities. Good teaching can provide an opportunity to discover one's thirst for and love of learning. Education is also a chance to discover one's own capability.

RELATIONSHIPS IN THE TEACHING SETTING

The relationship between teacher and student is central to Christian teaching. A hierarchical relationship lends itself to abuse. Those with power are likely to abuse that power by trying to control the students. Avoiding abuse of power requires that teachers and students respect one another and themselves. Respect for themselves allows students to retain power. Respect for students prevents teachers from claiming undue power over the students. Respect for teachers enables the students to hear with eager minds what is being said and to take the teachers' advice seriously. When the relationship between teacher and student is one of respect and care, then learning becomes a mutual task in which all participate and from which all benefit.

Because we live in a basically competitive culture, mutually beneficial participation in the teaching/learning process is difficult. When students are intent on proving their competence at the expense of one another, then competition is present in a destructive form. When teachers favor some students over others, then competition is inevitable. Competition encourages people to treat knowledge as a scarce commodity that can be won or lost but never shared.

Even Bible study can degenerate into a competitive activity. Those who know the most come to feel their superiority; the rest only sense their inadequacy. Those who win struggle endlessly to perform, to stay ahead of the rest; they exhaust themselves in the effort. Those who lose feel shame, embarrassment, and sorrow. The feelings of inadequacy may lead many people to give up on church educational opportunities. They settle for the information they already possess. Many adult Christians have no interest in Christian education for themselves, believing it necessary only for children. They seem to believe that Christian education is a need one outgrows. Too many adult Christians go through life with a fourth-grade understanding of the faith.

Every teaching moment can offer an opportunity for Christian growth, for Christian experience, and for Christian community. In such situations, learning is an activity in which everyone participates. The teacher acts as a catalyst for the process by encouraging every sign of growth. The teacher nudges every movement toward expression of an idea and supports those who dare to think in new ways. The teacher also gently leads the class to value the tradition highly, to consider it seriously, to understand and appreciate the way in which those who have gone before have reflected. A good teacher will not simply affirm every expressed idea but will affirm the students themselves as worthy persons, thereby helping students think critically and appreciatively.

LECTIO DIVINA

One good example of participatory teaching is the Bible teaching method known as *lectio divina* or "holy reading." This approach to scripture study seeks to encounter the living God through the text. The primary goal is not to gain information about the text but to appreciate the encounter between the text and the reader. In contrast to much content-centered Bible study, this method generally involves short passages that are read several times while paying close attention to how the words strike the hearts and minds of the hearers. For a more comprehensive look at this method, see Norvene Vest's book *Gathered in the Word: Praying the Scripture in Small Groups.* (See Appendixes I and II for her explanation of the process.)

In one form of lectio, the text is read four times: once to enable everyone to hear it, to recognize it, to pay attention. Then the second time the text is read, the leader asks the hearers to listen for words or phrases in the text that attract their attention, words or phrases that "shimmer" for the hearer, that raise questions or seem pivotal or that may be new in the hearing. One may hear the same text several times, and each time hear something new and different in very familiar words. During the third reading, the leader asks hearers to notice their emotional response to what they have heard, particularly to the word or phrase that caught their attention. Such responses may include thankfulness, joy, puzzlement, surprise, anger, disappointment, fear, delight, or amazement. With the fourth reading, the leader invites the hearers to notice what God is saying to them. This may come in the form of an invitation to be or do something, a challenge to current assumptions, a welcome relief in the form of confirmation of some direction taken, or another form of address. During his part of the process, the Bible may become a personal "word" from God.

After each of the three readings in which an assignment is made, the leader or teacher will encourage the group members to share their responses aloud. In the process of sharing, the students teach one another. The collective insights of several people will be much more complete than a single individual could possibly discover. Each person will discover his or her ability to grasp ideas and express them. This approach to Bible study can persuade persons that they can read the Bible with intelligence and have insights of value to offer others. The shared learning process makes it possible for people to study scripture without feeling either demeaned by their ignorance or the total irrelevance of the scriptural information. In this process the participants actually grow in their faith and Christian experience. As they learn together, they become a community of learning. Each one makes a valuable contribution to the others, and everyone's ideas count.

We know people remember only about twenty percent of what they hear, yet much education revolves around lengthy lectures. The teacher relays information, and the student struggles to remember some of it. People remember a higher percentage of what they see and explore for themselves than of words spoken to them. Students are far more likely to remember a passage of scripture that a leader used for *lectio* than one that formed the basis of a teacher's oral presentation. Teachers may feel good about themselves after they have waxed eloquent about a subject, but the primary question to ask is, Who benefited? The questions raised then are, Did the students grow? Did the teacher really teach? Has transformation occurred?

This method of Bible study energizes people because it involves them in their own new learning. The leader or pastor need not feel compelled to give too much information or to demonstrate superior knowledge. The leader may add information as is relevant or requested but carefully avoids taking over the process. The *lectio* process requires great discipline from the pastor who leads it. The pastor or teacher must believe that it is possible to learn *from* the students as well as *with* them.

SENSE OF BELONGING AS EDUCATION

Lectio is a good example for all church education. People may want new information, but they do not want it imposed on them by an expert who leaves them feeling dependent and ignorant. They want to be treated with dignity; they want to participate in their learning; they want to feel that they have some ability that matters.

For example, the point of a new members' class is not to overload people with information about church history or traditions. While they need some information in order to develop a sense of community and belonging, the new members' primary need is to acquaint themselves with other congregational members, the pastor, and congregational leaders. It may be necessary to limit the information presented, while allowing time for the class members to get to know one another. Only then will persons begin to feel that they belong and develop a sense that someone knows them, a sense that they are part of a caring community. As new members spend time together, tell their stories of faith, share experiences, and pray with one another, they become a community that offers what new members need most—a sense of belonging.

Providing such an opportunity is an educational process. It prepares them for their experience as church members, while possibly ensuring their continued church participation. Few persons leave the church because they do not have enough information; they leave because they do not feel they matter or because they have no friendship connections within the congregation.

Henri J. M. Nouwen wrote about what he called "redemptive education." Such education takes place when classes are settings "where community can be experienced, where people can live together without fear of each other, and learning can be based on a creative exchange of experiences and ideas."[4] A redemptive learning environment is one in which people mature in faith. Such growth is an essential part of the spiritual development process.

TEACHING AND SPIRITUAL GROWTH

The pastor as teacher is a potential guide for the spiritual growth of those who become students, whatever the teaching situation. Every student is a person who is on the journey to deepen faith, to grow closer to Jesus Christ, to express faith in the totality of life. In short, every student is seeking deeper intimacy with God and the understanding necessary to develop such intimacy. The effective teacher can guide the souls of students through this process. Every teaching moment is an opportunity for the growth in faith of those who learn.

All too often teachers allow the content of what they teach to distract them from the presence of those they teach. The content is important. Students enter into the teaching/learning situation with the legitimate expectation that what they learn in content will lead them to make new discoveries. Yet the content can become an idol so that even the well-meaning teacher engages in violent teaching, force-feeding the content to the students' minds and neglecting their being in the process.

The teacher must ask, What is the function of content? Do I teach for the sake of gratifying my own ego? to share what I know and to express my ideas? Or do I teach in order to invite the students into the adventure of learning? Does the content I offer inspire them to pursue further discovery? If the answer to the last question is yes, then real learning will take place. Students who are invited into the process of discovery for themselves will continue to learn after the class has ended. Those students who depend upon the teacher as dispenser of knowledge will stop growing. When the focus of the class is upon content as a catalyst for further learning, and not as an end in itself, then learning will continue.

The real content of every Christian education event is the

lives of the students. They bring their own faith, their desire to grow in discipleship, their life experience, and their enthusiasm for learning to the class. All of these contributions become the focus for education that takes them seriously and seeks to encourage them in their growth as disciples. Such education is a process of spiritual guidance. Lewis Joseph Sherrill has defined Christian education: "Christian education is the attempt, ordinarily by members of the Christian community, to participate in and to guide the changes which take place in persons in their relationships with God, with the church, with other persons, with the physical world, and with oneself."[5]

This definition clearly implies that Christian education is far more than imparting information; rather it is the transformation of persons. The teacher is not the transformer; the process of education led by the teacher enables that transformation to take place. The teacher is the guide for this spiritual change. The teacher enables persons to be open to the changes that, in the final analysis, are brought about by the work of the Holy Spirit.

TEACHING AS SPIRITUAL GUIDANCE

Prayer is the first necessary ingredient of teaching that has the character of spiritual guidance. The teacher grounds the content of the teaching session in prayer. The teacher prays for the presence of the Holy Spirit and for the Spirit's movement in the hearts and minds of all involved. The teacher also prays for the students, holding each before God. The students pray for the teacher and for themselves that together they may discover truth for themselves and grow in faith, no matter what the content. To the extent that prayer undergirds the whole process, miracles can take place, and students will learn—no matter what the content—something of what it means to be Christians.

Attention to the students is the second necessary ingredient in the process of teaching as spiritual guidance. The teacher patiently watches for signs that the students have grasped an idea, that truth has struck them, that they have found something that invites them to move deeper. The teacher dares to put content on hold occasionally in order to spend a moment encouraging a student, affirming that student's ability, challenging the student to take another step forward.

Resistance to learning signals the student's lack of readiness for what the teacher is presenting. The teacher may need to move more slowly, change the lesson plan, or adapt the material to the particular situation.

Spiritual guidance becomes part of the teaching process whenever the teacher pays sufficient attention to the students so that they not only learn the content, but they also learn to trust themselves, to feel confident in their ability to reflect, and to enjoy the delight of discovering new knowledge. For this to happen, the teacher's primary intention must be that of teaching students rather than teaching a particular subject. The teacher must observe the learning process and find ways to encourage that process.

Growth of the students themselves is the third ingredient of teaching as spiritual guidance. One measure of effective teaching in the church is the quality of faith of class members. Study should produce a difference in the life of faith. The teacher models faith by demonstrating a pastoral and caring concern for the students. At its best, learning is a process of expanding one's horizons. Learning enables people to express their faith with greater clarity, thus giving them more confidence in that faith.

Teachers may assist the students in the process of transformation, but they cannot make it happen. Teachers cannot force or control the process, nor through teaching can teachers manipulate learners into becoming the persons God has created them to be. Ultimately the miracle of human growth and transformation happens through the work of the Holy Spirit.

Teaching as a form of care is the fourth way teaching becomes spiritual guidance. The teacher reaches out to the students, pays attention to their questions, follows their struggles with sensitivity, and views them as whole persons. Students bring their life situations to the class with all the attendant joy or sorrow. Inattention, difficulty with new ideas, stress, or boredom may indicate more than meets the eye; these symptoms may indicate problems at home or work, or some other area of brokenness. The students are hurting in various ways and are simply unable to be receptive. The caring teacher will notice this and follow up by asking questions outside of the classroom. A note or phone call expressing concern may break through resistance, enabling the student to move forward in new ways. When the teacher ignores these clues and pushes ahead with the prepared material, the content may be presented properly but the students will not learn.

Christian faith has a necessary content that teachers must convey. Education is not a luxury for Christians who seek to grow. But learning the faith happens in a variety of ways: through words in a lecture or book, from shared learning in discussion, by following role models, by acting out faith. Students learn by engaging in the act of worship, by learning prayers in the process of praying with other believers. As they learn, they reflect their growth in deepening faith, which allows them to become more fully what God wants them to be in Christ. Good education may not answer all the questions; it may only increase the questions. But good education will give students an appropriate sense of trust in the community of faith, in those who lead them, and in themselves as learners.

Every pastor is a teacher. Every pastor can be a spiritual guide also in the process of teaching by paying attention to students, by concentrating on their needs, by involving them in the learning/teaching experience, and by helping them experience their own power as participants rather than as passive receivers. Every teaching situation is an opportunity for spiritual guidance: A group of disciples is voluntarily present, eager and waiting for the movement of the Holy Spirit.

The teacher serves as the spiritual guide for this group as the teacher prayerfully approaches the teaching task with the understanding that the growth of persons is the central goal of what takes place. Teaching involves both the transmission of knowledge and the use of the teaching/learning process to foster persons' growth. Learning will take place when teachers view students as disciples who want to grow in faith and understanding. The teacher serves the students best when the teacher loves them and wills their wholeness.

Christian education began as a process for the formation of disciples. The early church involved converts to Christianity in a lengthy process of catechesis. They learned the creeds, prayers, and scriptures of the faith, thereby preparing them for their baptism, the ultimate goal of the process. On the evening before Easter, these prepared converts gathered at the church. They were stripped of their clothing, dipped in the water, and given new clothes and new names. Then they received an invitation to partake of the sacrament of Holy Communion. Their identity was changed in the process.

Christian education can still be about the same process of making and forming disciples. The miracle of grace can form disciples in the classroom, living room, or any other setting where Christian education takes place. To the extent that the teacher and the students expect the miracle of transformation to happen, pray for it, encourage it, and watch for it, transformation will take place today just as it did in the second century. The pastor as teacher will serve as the midwife of this newly transformed life, acting as the spiritual guide for those who learn.

CHAPTER SEVEN

Social Change as Spiritual Guidance

T HE CHRISTIAN CHURCH has been an essential leaven for justice and truth and has often served to change oppressive
structures in any society. Such was certainly true of the
work of American churches during the decade of the 1960s in
the struggle for legal civil rights in America. The pronounce-
ments of churches, the activities of pastors and laypeople in
marching, protesting, and seeking justice had a profound impact
upon the political landscape. Some of the enemies of racial inte-
gration acknowledged that without the support of churches
and their efforts, resistance might have succeeded.

During that exciting decade, I served as the pastor of an
urban church in the inner city of Chicago. As I reflect on our
work, I am amazed at what one small congregation was able to
accomplish. We founded the first community-chartered credit
union so neighborhood people could save money and take out
loans for home improvements in a community that had been
blacklisted by banks. We organized the first bilingual Head Start
program for preschool children. With the help of other churches and the local community organization, we challenged the

political leadership of the city and rezoned a part of the neighborhood to preserve its residential character. Churches are not helpless; they can make a significant difference in their communities.

We live today in a time of reaction and withdrawal from issues of social justice. The social changes of the 1960s and 1970s seem to frighten rather than encourage American society. Churches reflect more societal norms than they may believe, often behaving much like the society in which they operate. Like society at large, churches may find themselves reacting to their own previous involvements. Many churches have turned inward, concentrating upon recovery of their life, their denominational identity, their structures. As mirrors of society at large, churches have tried to distance themselves from the decades of social change.

FALSE ASSUMPTIONS ABOUT SPIRITUALITY

Unfortunately, one of the unwitting allies of this inward focus has been spirituality. Often people have used spiritual renewal events and retreats as an excuse to avoid dealing with difficult social issues. Frequently spirituality has been presented and understood as an intentional withdrawal from activity to focus on relationship with God. Spirituality's current popularity results in part from the idea that deeply religious persons can avoid involvement in the messy world.

A definition of spirituality that negates people's involvement in society's affairs bases itself on several false assumptions. These assumptions separate spirituality from action in the world. They have contributed to the increasing isolation of churches from society and the church's irrelevance to societal issues. For churches to emerge from this isolation, some false understandings of the nature of Christian spirituality have to change. The basic assumptions about spirituality we need to challenge are these:

1. Spirituality is solely or primarily a matter between an individual and God. Other people get in the way of the individual's experience of God or at best contribute nothing to that relationship.

2. Spirituality is best nurtured with as little to do with the physical body as possible. Physical objects and needs interfere with one's relationship with God; they are distractions to be ignored.

3. Spirituality has to do with matters between the soul and God. Issues such as economics or politics can serve as tempting distractions that cause a person to abandon the search for God. A goal of the spiritual life is distance from the world, its temptations and its problems.

4. The spiritual life is a matter of being rather than doing. One must learn to stop activity and settle down to pray and be still.

Each of these four assumptions, while containing a kernel of truth, contributes to a false kind of spirituality. Each also contributes to an abandonment of mission and leaves the world in the hands of scoundrels.

1 *The assumption of the dichotomy of individual and community* needs to be questioned. While affirming the validity of experience of God, encounters with God are more than private affairs. The scriptures bear witness to the importance of divine encounter with people in groups.

No one can be a Christian in isolation. Human beings need to be in relationship with other people. God is to be found in the connections made between people and among people in groups. The church provides opportunities for communal experiences in which persons may find God in human relationships. Even the most annoying people may serve as instruments through whom God can work. Their presence can force reconsideration and growth—challenging us and pushing us toward new self-discovery. Pleasant, affirming, and agreeable people may not help us grow, but they provide much-needed support in times of crisis. They carry us when we cannot carry ourselves.

This assertion about the importance of other people for spiritual growth has a great deal to do with social action in the world. Most of the time we live in narrow worlds with people much like ourselves. Encounters are generally pleasant and nonthreatening. For most of us, such experiences of peaceful encounter are necessary most of the time. We can handle only a minimal amount of conflict and disagreement. Yet if we surround ourselves with people and situations that affirm and do not challenge, growth will not take place.

As wonderful as comfort and ease may be, spiritual growth most often happens when something or someone rubs our edges, questions our boundaries, and challenges our assumptions. Spiritual growth most likely will take place when we find ourselves pushed into new and unfamiliar experiences, when familiar grounding is disturbed, when routines are broken. In these spaces our defenses do not work; our habitual responses are insufficient; and our need for God becomes most real. When other people and events jar life from its moorings, our need for God becomes genuine and apparent.

We can learn a great deal from those times when life falls apart because we have to start over without the comfort of predictable answers, without the security of having clues to the future. Chaos drives us to our knees. Trouble opens doors into the depth of our souls, the place where we are most likely to encounter God. Instead of fleeing difficult issues or fearing possible conflict, we can learn to recognize that our greatest spiritual growth may take place at our levels of greatest discomfort caused by other people.

2 *The assumption that spiritual growth is removed from the physical world* divides spirit from flesh. God made no mistake in creating the physical universe. We cannot separate the human body from the spirit without damage to both body and spirit. Biblical witness attests that God created bodies as part of the good creation; thus bodies serve as proper means through which divine encounter takes place. Christians celebrate this unity of flesh and spirit in the heart of faith as the Incarnation: Jesus Christ, God in human flesh. Affirming belief in the Incarnation forces us to take flesh seriously as a sign of God's presence.

People have often recognized encounters with God through bodily experiences. Physical healings exemplify the body as a sign of God's presence. The realization that prayer, laying on of hands, anointing with oil, or some other means have brought about a physical healing serves to acknowledge the connection between body and spirit. Other physical experiences that convey God's presence include visions and voices. In both experiences, God meets the believer through the means of the physical body. Though these experiences are unusual, most people respond to them with awe.

Many more Christians have less dramatic encounters with God related to their bodies. Some know what it is to be awakened from sleep in the middle of the night—restless and unable to return to sleep; in those moments they know that God has called them to do something. Others know the experience of fasting as an aid to prayer. The physical body is changed by the experience of fasting, and the effect upon prayer is sometimes dramatic. Still others have experienced the power of body posture in prayer. Kneeling, for example, may bring about depths in prayer that remain unexperienced while sitting or standing.

A spirituality that takes the body seriously dares to take the bodies of other people seriously also. Feeding the hungry and clothing the naked are spiritual activities. We tend to think of these activities as less spiritual than prayer, but the Christian church has understood the need for all of these acts of mercy as spiritual disciplines. For this reason, the church consistently has named forms of ministry that deal with all parts of human life as equally spiritual. When we engage in such spiritual activities, we open a window to the divine. We discover the reality of God in the person of those most in need.

3 *The third assumption about the separation between the religious and the secular* requires careful reconsideration. The notion of an arbitrary division between an arena called sacred and the rest of life really began with the Enlightenment in the late seventeenth century. Only after the rise of secularism as a philosophy have people considered that any arena of life is unrelated to God. Before that time, life was understood as a whole: God's involvement included every human activity, from plowing a field to writing a poem.

The original intention of the isolation and designation of life's arenas, such as economics, politics, employment, and sexuality, as secular was to free people from church control. For example, the understanding of politics as a secular activity emerged in order to liberate politics from the constraints and control of the clergy. Democratic political life needed that liberation in order to flourish. American liberty may not have been possible without some separation of church and state. And some credit is due to those who helped free arenas of life from clerical control.

Persons who have been inspired by a beautiful piece of secular music or who have found God's presence in a work experience know the limitation of this division between sacred and secular. We cannot limit God to religious matters. God, as creator of the universe, is greater than any human creation. The real danger of this arbitrary separation is that it may prevent persons from being open to God in a great many of their experiences. Because they do not believe they can discover God outside their narrow world of the sacred, their spirits are closed. They miss the discovery of God in other places in their lives.

Breaking down the wall between sacred and secular enables us to discover God and God's leading in every arena of life. The adventure of discipleship includes church and government, economics and employment. This broad understanding enables persons to notice God and to follow God into the world.

4 *The assumption that the spiritual life is passive rather than active* poses another challenge. This assumption fosters an essentially selfish spirituality: We become the focus of our spirituality, not God. We measure all experiences through our feelings. Such a spirituality has little in common with historic Christian faith.

People can exhaust themselves by ceaselessly doing good. Activity as an end in itself can drain us of our vitality. Some have found themselves depleted by work for social justice and have retreated into a highly privatized form of spirituality, reacting their way into a spirituality of retreat. Christian life exhausted in activity may result in a passive form of discipleship.

The Christian life is meant to reflect a balance, achieved through a rhythm both of doing and of being. If we engage in endless activity without pauses for rest, prayer, and reflection, we will exhaust ourselves. On the other hand, complete concentration on prayer and silence without accompanying action causes us to get stuck in ourselves, and our lives become irrelevant to the world.

For the sake of believers, spirituality must include what we do as well as how we are, include acts of mercy as much as prayer. Any spiritual practice that opens persons to God is useful and good, and we discover God in the midst of activity on behalf of others. That is at least one meaning behind Jesus' words, "Inasmuch as you do it to one of the least of these my sister and brother, you do it to me." To focus all one's spiritual energy inward is to miss meeting Christ in the person of the one who is needy.

These four assumptions restrict spirituality in ways that damage the believer and hamper the clear connection between spirituality and doing justice. An important part of the pastoral task rests in challenging these assumptions and helping parishioners do the same. The challenge may not be verbal; it may be by example. Pastors who demonstrate a broad spirituality in their lives will model that breadth for others, who may not know how. Once they have seen the pastor in action, they may discover that doing justice is not frightening; it does not set them apart from God in some secular realm. Instead they find that acts of faithfulness bring them closer to God.

DANGERS CONNECTED WITH SOCIAL CHANGE

Pastors and other Christians expose themselves to danger when they assume the role of change agent. One danger is allowing pride to demean everyone who does not share our particular passion for solutions to the world's problems as somehow less than faithful to the gospel. We attach our egos to our particular solutions to the world's ills and in so doing, we harshly judge all who may seek other avenues toward the same goal. Self-righteousness may be the single greatest sin of those who care deeply about social change.

The danger of anger exists. Working with social problems that do not go away and with people who do not improve may generate anger out of frustration. Many prophetic people's level of anger can spoil their good intentions. Anger can distract attention from the issue that needs change. People resent their anger, and that resentment shows up in resistance to the proposed solution.

A third danger is the abuse of power by trying to control other people. The would-be prophet may direct social action toward specific changes when persuaded of the need to control situations and people. If persons believe that they are right and on the side of God, then they may easily conclude that the importance of their conviction overrides other people's opposition. Because power exists for use, it is tempting to enjoy the use of power too much and to become addicted to having and exercising power.

The three temptations of pride, anger, and power have spoiled the good intentions, the noble ambitions, and the potential achievements of many religious leaders. Fear of this distortion of discipleship frequently causes the cautious spirit to back away from involvement in social action.

The danger of *not* being involved is even greater. We may avoid the temptations of anger, power, and pride; but in the process, we may give in to the evils that operate freely when good people offer no opposition. Good people's preoccupation with their own souls means the poor and helpless people of the world suffer from lack of someone to advocate for them, to speak on their behalf, or to serve them in their need. We good people can lose our own souls when we forget that we find God through service to the poor and needy. Doing justice is not a luxury for people who want to develop a spiritual life. We encounter God whenever and wherever we engage the world's pain.

The pastor who would be the spiritual guide for the congregation cannot bless escape from the world. Efforts at escape are unfaithful to the gospel, and they isolate people from the One they seek. To be an honest and faithful spiritual guide, the pastor must help individuals and the congregation as a whole face the world with courage and hope, seeking avenues to make the world more human and more humane.

THE PASTOR'S ROLE

Every function of pastoral ministry provides an opportunity to present the gospel challenge. Worship, pastoral care, teaching and organizational life: All are settings for guidance and for the presentation of justice issues as opportunities to serve God. In each setting, the pastor can do at least three things: challenge the people with the gospel message, help them discover concrete ways to make a difference, and offer them hope that their efforts are acceptable to God.

Worship is the most natural setting to present the challenge of the gospel. While preaching is the most obvious vehicle for portraying the challenges of the gospel to our world, the entire worship service can open people to new forms of service and new windows for reflection on God's world. Hymns, prayers, scripture, litanies can all serve to present the gospel challenge. This challenge should be advanced without appealing to guilt. Most people do not respond well to guilt as motivation for change. Attitudes and behavior are more likely to change when people perceive the challenge as a vision of the possible. An invitation offered with warmth and graciousness welcomes the people and challenges them to follow Christ into the world with a sense of joy. One-to-one pastoral care also offers opportunities to express the challenge. Those people who need to be drawn out of themselves will especially benefit from this form of challenge.

Pastors also guide parishioners to discover ways they may act responsibly as Christ's people in the world. Some leaders give people solutions that represent the personal agenda of the leader. The people either accept the leader's direction and follow blindly, or they resist. Either reaction denies people responsibility for their own actions. Leadership that takes responsibility away from people by making decisions for them does not lead to spiritual growth. Only when people consider real options and make decisions based on those possibilities can they take adult responsibility for their lives. Even if the form of service involves sacrifice, the people will have chosen it for themselves rather than being browbeaten into doing it.

As servants of the community of Christ, pastors must trust persons to make good decisions. Pastors do not have all the answers, and we must not pretend that we do. The problems of the world are complex; they defy easy solutions. No single person can come to the best solution single-handed. The collective wisdom of a group of people may unearth a better solution than any one person could. The process of mutual discovery of that collective wisdom is central to all efforts to change society.

Pastors contribute to spiritual growth when we affirm members' contributions as valuable and acceptable; we negate

spiritual growth when we make them feel that their contributions are not worthwhile. Henri J. M. Nouwen insisted that
shared responsibility is at the heart of genuine social change.
He challenged Christian leaders to take the wisdom of the
people seriously: "We are used to saying to people that they
have responsibilities. To say that they also have the authority
which goes with it, however, is something else."[1] Authority for
change belongs to all the people, but belief in that authority
requires trust in their wisdom, faithfulness, and intelligence.

When congregational members find that the pastor really
believes in them and takes their ideas seriously, then the process
of mutual discovery can take place. When permitted to make
good decisions and encouraged to follow through on their own
best instincts, people are often more ready and eager to take
concrete action on behalf of others.

Pastors hold out a vision of hope to the people. Too often
the enemy of change is discouragement. People give up when
their efforts do not produce the desired results. They are discouraged when others do not respond to their efforts with
appreciation and when solutions do not seem to make a difference. When people lose hope, they give up the effort. One
reason for the lack of social passion in our society and church
today is that persons sense that all the good ideas and action
plans of the past two or three decades have done no good and
may have made things worse.

When pastors offer hope, people can see even small victories in the light of a greater vision; they can discover creative
energy for further work in the joy of accomplishment and the
sense that what they have done matters. Hope is an attitude
that does not depend upon specific results. All who work for
social change must have specific results in mind; but when faith
informs the vision, hope can survive the knowledge of failure

in specific situations. Hope does not depend upon results; hope holds fast to the belief that only God knows the meaning of events. Only from an eternal perspective can the value of results be understood. Hope is the willingness to trust in God and to believe that God can be found in the future. This hope can persist whatever the circumstances or the results.

Pastors continually need to offer hope as parishioners attempt to live faithfully. We can offer this hope in sermons, in teaching, in counseling, in leadership situations. Ministry must always be a proclamation of good news: the good news that God loves the world, God is at work in the world to bring about justice. Our labor for justice is in accord with God's will. Whatever we do in harmony with God's intention is not wasted effort, however unclear the results. Pastors remind the faithful of the fruitfulness of their efforts in the long run.

The call to action in the world begins with challenge. The pastoral task is to disturb people with the truth of how things are in the world, to remind them of human suffering and injustice, and to encourage them to take risks to make a difference. But the pastoral task begins with the proclamation of hope and vision grounded in God's love for the world.

The pastor as spiritual guide enables the congregation to grasp the truth about the need for personal involvement in making the world a better place for all. Part of the task of spiritual guidance is to help people break free from narrow confines of selfishness, moving them to risk for others. At times the pastor must be the dreamer of great dreams for the whole community of faith, the one who dares to pose possibilities that others have not yet considered.

Yet every pastor realizes how remarkably resistant to change most people are. Argument and logic will rarely produce change. John R. Fry has written, "People do not change. They act and react. They are forced either to adopt new ideas by pressures brought to bear on them in their life situation, or else to resist these pressures with unmeasured willfulness."[2] Pressuring people to "think as I do" will only increase their resistance.

Giving members opportunities to experience life from the perspective of the hurting and the poor is a highly effective way to develop sensitivity to these issues. Serving as adult sponsors for a work camp in Mexico can do more to change attitudes toward developing nations than sermons and lectures. Serving meals one day a month in a neighborhood soup kitchen can do more to change attitudes toward poverty and homelessness than sermons could ever do. A great blessing of pastoral ministry is witnessing the transformation that can occur when people see for themselves the world's injustice and realize they can participate in changes.

Poverty, racism, prejudice, underemployment, homelessness, lack of equal opportunity are all present in American society. Part of the pastoral task is to name and identify these evils. The people harmed by these evils are often voiceless; they depend upon the voice of pastors and other religious leaders. Those who participate in the injustice by doing nothing need the challenge and transformation. Pastors act as spiritual leaders and guides when we present and address society's needs. Helping people encounter the risen Christ in the faces of the poor is as much an act of spiritual guidance as teaching them to pray.

CHAPTER EIGHT

Management as Spiritual Guidance

THE LIFE OF EVERY congregation finds expression in two primary ways: through worship and in meetings. The church is an institution, and at times every pastor functions as an administrator of the institution. Church administration is accomplished through the tasks of the preparation for, staffing, and follow-up of meetings. Meetings are necessary if the work of the church is to belong to the people. Otherwise, it becomes the work of the staff and will not receive the congregation's enthusiastic support. Meetings are necessary because the collective wisdom of several voices is better than a single one. We meet for many different purposes: planning, educating, setting policy, dealing with personnel issues, praying, raising funds, getting acquainted—to name only a few. Meetings are not irrelevant to the faith. What happens in meetings may be as important as any other event in determining the quality of the shared life of the people.

Whenever a group meets in the church, a part of the beloved community gathers for a stated purpose. Many people know that growth occurs in small groups that meet for study and prayer; however, every church meeting can be an occasion that enables persons to experience and express the power of God's grace and presence. Every meeting should be an opportunity for the spiritual growth of those present and, through them, for the whole congregation.

Although the practice of individual spiritual direction is growing rapidly among Protestants, the form of spiritual direction that has marked Protestantism most is that of small groups. Both the English Puritans and the Continental Pietists grounded their spirituality and practice in small groups or covenant communities that met regularly for prayer, for sharing God's work in their lives, for mutual support and encouragement, and sometimes for correction of error or sin. Thomas Shepard, a Puritan leader, set forth the purpose of private small group meetings as serving as channels for the Holy Spirit. He listed six ways these meetings could function:

1) Christians in small groups could more easily express love to one another,

2) these groups could be communities of prayer,

3) members could apply the gospel to one another and thus assist one another,

4) members could teach one another,

5) the group could comfort the sad or those in mourning,

6) the group could serve as a forum in which members could learn to express their faith and the gifts of the Spirit more boldly.[1]

John Wesley organized the Methodist movement around similar small groups. The Methodist small group, or class, provided a safe, accepting place. These classes nurtured faith, heard confession, shared thanksgivings, provided correction and discipline, and upheld one another in prayer. Wesley stated his design and rationale for the classes in these words:

> There are about twelve persons in every class, one of whom is styled *the Leader*. It is his business:
>
> (1). To see each person in his class once a week at the least; in order
>
> To receive what they are willing to give toward the relief of the poor;
>
> To inquire how their souls prosper;
>
> To advise, reprove, comfort, or exhort, as occasion may require.[2]

Each week the Leader brought the work of his class to the steward of the society. In this way pastoral care over the whole society was exercised.

These Wesleyan groups shaped a unique people who were deeply committed to a renewal of their life with God. That interior life expressed itself in their dealings with others. These classes provided the power behind the early Methodist movement and were Methodism's major contribution to small-group ministry and the practice of group spiritual direction.

While we are only now rediscovering the value of the small group, many examples throughout contemporary Protestant history attest to its power. Many Bible study groups are actually informal spiritual direction groups. People attend less for the new knowledge about scripture and more for the support and encouragement of the group. Pastoral efforts to enhance the study program by introducing more structured materials may meet strong resistance; study is the catalyst for the group but not its most important purpose. Many people attend because they are lonely, and the study-group members give them a sense that they matter in an increasingly impersonal world. The sense of community draws them to the group.

The Religious Society of Friends has continued the practice of group direction in several forms. Worship itself is a form of group direction; persons freely bring their contribution and sit in prayerful silence as the group helps the individual discern a divine leading. A special form of group spiritual direction among Friends is what they call "clearness committees." These groups have a particular focus to assist a member who is seeking the Spirit's leading. The person asks for a meeting of the committee to gain assistance in making an important decision. The committee helps the member by asking questions rather than by giving advice. Their questions help focus a member's attention on his or her life and the Spirit's leading. The Religious Society of Friends assumes that the right questions will bring the person's wisdom to the fore. The person then may probe for the answers already present. The committee members also pray for the individual during the process of providing group spiritual guidance. The clearness committee enables the individual to make careful decisions about possible options.

African American churches developed a method of group support to withstand the pressures of living in a racist society. These groups have continued into this century. The elders gather to assist those wavering in the faith. These elders become role models to the young or to those new to the faith. The elders often serve as prayer warriors on behalf of the whole community. They offer advice when weaker members are in danger of accommodating worldly ways. Often an elder is assigned to a new believer at his or her baptism, and the elder follows that person's growth for a long period of time. Together the elders provide group guidance to the congregation.

The elders also may meet as individuals with others whom they believe to be in trouble, offering the wisdom of their guidance. Howard Thurman, in his autobiography *With Head and Heart*, writes about one such elder, a somewhat severe but helpful guide to him shortly after his baptism. Thurman was fishing and fighting against a strong wind when he fell and hit his head against the seat of the boat. He uttered profanities and then proceeded to cry. His spiritual elder said to him, "Let that be an object lesson to you....Satan is always waiting to tempt you to make you turn your back on your Lord." In reflecting on the situation, Thurman writes,

> Looking back, it is clear to me that the watchful attention of my sponsors in the church served to enhance my consciousness that whatever I did with my life mattered. They added to the security given to me by the quiet insistence of my mother and especially by my grandmother that their children's lives were a precious gift.[3]

The twelve-step movement has taken the best of group direction and used it to provide a process that moves people from addiction to freedom. Central to every twelve-step meeting is honesty. People attempt to speak the hard and painful truth without excuses. These groups are amazingly accepting because each member is also an addict. No one sits in judgment. Many people who have been freed from addiction through a twelve-step program return occasionally to such a group wherever they may travel. The honesty and intimacy of the group is a life-and-death matter! People do not fail to attend their group meetings. They know that sanity and sobriety depend upon their attendance.

The Upper Room's Walk to Emmaus practices an ongoing small-group discipline. The Emmaus community refers to the small groups that meet regularly as Fourth Day or reunion groups. These groups grow out of an initial Thursday through Sunday experience, which is intensely powerful and often life changing. Both Cursillo and the Walk to Emmaus programs have recognized that without a follow-up group to provide continued support, the initial experience will fade away. The small group becomes a base for ongoing encouragement, prayerful support, and accountability. Many Christians affirm the renewal of their faith through participation in such an intentional community.

Even in small congregations, people may not know one another well. They make every effort to avoid speaking about anything personal, especially anything that suggests that one is not completely happy and successful. Thus, a person who is going through hell over the sexual behavior of a teenage child may endure the pain quietly. Rather than seeking help for the problem or strength through the prayers and encouragement of others, the person is isolated and alone in the struggle. The pastor may be the only person who knows the situation of many in the room. They really do not know one another, and they cannot pray for one another or offer help because they are afraid to reveal their secrets and sorrows.

If members of the faith community do not feel free to express what is most important to them, they cannot be fully themselves; they will wear masks to shield or hide themselves from others. The masks will get in the way of everything they do. Many congregational leaders believe that more meetings and more small groups are the way to break through isolation and lack of intimacy. Yet more meetings do not promote intimacy. Increasing the number of contacts may produce even more pain as a result of false contact that lacks depth. Isolated and lonely people feel even more helpless when in contact with others and unable to benefit from that contact. Nowhere is this more true than when we call the activities "fellowship." When persons attend a "fellowship" event and still feel lonely, their pain increases.

In our highly mobile culture, loneliness is a painful reality for many people. The small group is a necessary form of ministry. The persistence of many forms of small-group ministry in the church—often without official support or encouragement—indicates their importance. In some instances, entire congregations organize around the small-group model. Small groups enable large congregations to provide personal support for members who might otherwise get lost. Yet even small congregations are too big to provide the kind of intimacy that the small group can offer. The number of intentional small groups is growing today as people discover that their loneliness is a primary need, greater than their need for anonymity.

Sometimes churches set up special spiritual growth groups for the sole purpose of providing some form of group spiritual direction. Members join the group fully aware of what to expect. They will set aside time for their own spiritual growth and will expect the group to help them. People in most congregations are ready to deepen their spiritual lives and share their experiences of God's movement with those who want help from others. Tilden H. Edwards says that "at any one time there is a small group of people ready for such a serious group in any religious community (and in the larger community, as well). Such people are at a particular point of openness and vulnerability in relation to their deeper self in God."[4] A group organized for spiritual growth or group direction may answer that need.

PLANNING FOR SPIRITUAL GROWTH

Any group can become a setting that fosters spiritual growth. A group with a particular task to accomplish such as a governing council or a board of deacons may be such a setting, or it may be a church school teachers' group. To help its members most effectively, group membership needs some longevity so that people do not come and go too frequently. It make take several meetings to develop trust that leads to deeper conversation. It may take a year or more before people feel comfortable enough to share their joys and pains with others. People accustomed to keeping quiet about their personal lives will not suddenly start talking about themselves. Their resistance deserves respect. However, the group needs to understand its new role as facilitator of spiritual growth. People who join or are recruited for one purpose and who then discover this additional purpose may feel manipulated. Without genuine agreement that is neither rushed nor forced, some people will worry about the neglect of business matters, while others may resent any attention paid to business at all.

As a group engages in a process of exploration that invites members to share regularly the signs of God's presence in their lives, it may become evident that the group cannot serve two purposes easily. A church board may decide to create a spiritual growth group for those who wish to go deeper than is possible in the context of a business meeting agenda.

A decision to create a new group may avoid the problem of competitive agendas but will bring new problems. Will people make personal decisions about which group to join on the basis of their need? Will one group continue to work on business and the other withdraw to focus upon group members' needs? The potential for damaging division must be acknowledged at the beginning. The pastoral task is to help the members sort through the consequences of the decision. The pastor may be the only one who can help the group surface expectations as well as potential problems. The pastor will try to avoid group formation based upon we/they lines. Those who choose to belong to the growth group may depict those who do not as slackers. Those who choose to deepen their religious life by engaging in a process of group spiritual direction may perceive the others as less serious or devout. The pastor can help ensure that the decision takes into account all factors.

Three key ingredients foster spiritual growth in small groups. Spiritual growth happens when

1. *People are given a safe environment* in which to explore the inner life. Safety comes from trust that one will not be violated by criticism, that one's voice will be heard and openly received, and that confidentiality will be preserved. Most spiritual growth groups will need to have a formal means of ensuring a covenant of confidentiality. In some form, the covenant serves as a promise to respect what is spoken and to keep it within the group. Such a covenant may be printed and signed by all participants.

   In every group, especially one that is at work on an agenda, some tend to talk too much. The leader may need to take a fairly assertive stance to insist that the group observe times of silence. Just before or after a vote is a good time for silence. The silence may enable participants to discover what is calling them, what makes them uncomfortable, what may soften their hearts and even change their minds. The silence can make it possible for people to pay attention to the leading of the Spirit in the group. People need silence in order to pay attention to what is going on with their souls. Space for silence is probably the single most important ingredient for group spiritual development.

   The leader's role is to pay close attention to what is said as well as to what is not said. The leader needs to watch the way persons' body language indicates their level of participation in the group. The body language of an angry person may express feelings more accurately than any spoken words. Careful observation may give the leader additional information about spiritual needs. Often people will "check out" if a question makes them uncomfortable or hits too close to home or when a discussion topic distresses them. The pastor/leader has a dual role of paying attention to group process while watching for signs from individuals that may be calls for help. As a follow-up to verbal and nonverbal clues offered during the meeting, the pastor will want to hold the person in prayer or visit with the person at a later time. Because of the demands of this dual role, it may be wise to have one person chair the meeting and another to act as group spiritual director.

2. *Group members are encouraged to share* something of what is going on in their souls. Begin each meeting with a check-in time that may facilitate this process. Such check-in time also enables group members to understand why one person may seem dispirited or somewhat removed from the discussion at a given meeting or why another seems more talkative than usual. The pastor can set the example by sharing some of his or her own feelings, thus making it easier for others to follow. Times of sharing have to be non-coercive; people should not be forced to disclose more than is comfortable. The goal is a regular time at the beginning of each meeting when all have the opportunity to share what is foremost in their minds. This sharing introduces a process of noticing, and people begin to pay attention to one another and to hold one another in prayer.

A deeper form of sharing is the telling of life stories. This approach might begin at an initial retreat as the group begins a new year of work together. Setting aside retreat time clearly affirms personal spiritual development as one of the group's purposes. More progress toward the development of trust can take place in one full day of retreat than in several meetings over many months. The key is to begin life-story sharing when time is plentiful. The pastor should begin by sharing from his or her experience. Some pastors feel that it helps to preview the sharing exercise with one or two others to help the group process.

3. *People receive some spiritual growth content* from the pastor or another group member. A teaching occasion can revitalize the meeting and cause people to leave saying, "It was worth it to be here." This spiritual growth content could take the form of Bible study or teaching on various spiritual practices such as centering prayer or the Jesus prayer. Whatever the teaching, the purpose is to lead the participants into a deepening of their relationship to Jesus Christ.

DEALING WITH CHURCH MEETINGS

Transforming meetings into spiritual growth opportunities is a tall order given the rather humdrum nature of most church meetings. So often meetings are draining experiences that nearly everyone dreads and attends out of duty. Many people would rather be any place besides the current meeting, and the pastor may be among those.

Perhaps as pastors and Christian leaders we need to ask: Does this meeting really need to take place? If the answer is no, then we need to cancel the meeting or suggest a redirection. Going through the motions of a meeting simply because it is the third Tuesday of the month risks making the meeting a meaningless event. Most people would gladly receive a phone call informing them of the meeting's cancellation. The free evening is a gift. Most churches overorganize and operate with a more complicated structure than is necessary. Canceling unnecessary meetings might create more respect for and anticipation of the meetings that actually take place.

A second question to ask is this: How might leaders conduct this meeting so that those present grow in faith? This question differs from the usual one: How might leaders conduct the meeting so as to efficiently accomplish the necessary business? However, the two questions are not mutually exclusive. An inefficient meeting may cause frustration or even anger and thus block any kind of spiritual growth. For a meeting to have a chance at being a growth opportunity, it needs a clear purpose backed by careful planning and structure. Spiritual growth seldom occurs when people think they are wasting their time.

Much discussion in meetings has less to do with the task before the group than it does with what is going on in the lives of the participants. If the meeting focuses only on business to the exclusion of the needs and concerns of those present, people will find ways to get their own issues dealt with around the edges of the business, sometimes causing delays by sidetracking the intended issues. For those persons who express their feelings easily, this desire may reflect itself in belligerence over a minor detail. The real issue is the anger or frustration the participant has brought from work or home. An argument over what seems like a technicality may be the person's only way to express his or her anger.

Shy persons may respond differently. They may sit quietly, allowing anger to build up within and going home with a sense that their presence was not valued and their time was wasted. They will express their anger in mutterings to spouses or friends after the meeting. They do not openly subvert the process during the meeting, but they may hinder implementation of the results. Their resistance takes the shape of quiet withdrawal and nonparticipation in the proceedings.

Most business meetings follow some form of *Robert's Rules of Order*. This manual for procedures helps achieve order and fairness in meetings. After acknowledging this benefit from the use of the manual, we should also acknowledge that these "rules" do not always help a group function in humane ways. Because parliamentary procedures concentrate on orderly methods and equal time for varying points of view, persons receive little or no attention. These procedures do not foster spiritual growth.

A major limitation of such procedures is that they encourage a division between those in favor and those against a given proposal. Charles M. Olsen, in his landmark work on the behavior of church boards, remarks that this process "does not allow for the wisdom that can come from nonassertive, nonverbal people or from those whose wisdom is more intuitive and takes time to emerge. The process 'rushes to judgment' with little space for prayerful patience."[5] The church needs another process to do its business that doesn't abandon its commitment to persons and their value. Most of the members present do not contribute to the debate. Highly verbal, strongly opinionated people may dominate discussion. Their verbal expression may enforce the belief that what they have to say is more important than the thoughts of the quieter members.

Just because church members meet together a great deal does not mean that anyone benefits from these meetings. The business that gets done often bears little relationship to the time spent. A minor decision that has minimal budget implications can take the better part of an evening to settle. Everyone gets angry or frustrated in the process. When this experience becomes a pattern, people begin to dread the next meeting. They either find an excuse for not attending or go through the motions of attending but with a lowered sense of expectation.

They put in their time out of duty but anticipate that little of consequence will happen because of their presence.

Church boards are a primary source of discontent and frustration. We might think that serving on a board or church committee would be an opportunity for spiritual growth. Those who initially agree to serve may have had such expectations. Surely spending quality time with the pastor and other congregational leaders will promote faith and inspiration. Such service often disappoints board members; their expectations remain unmet. In his book *Transforming Church Boards*, Charles M. Olsen reports the results of a survey of former church officers: "In response to an open-ended question about what surprised them, 155 registered positive responses, while 199 registered negative responses. Twenty-nine percent reported that they were weary and burned out."[6]

People go home from meetings exhausted, frustrated, or angry but not spiritually fed. At the end of their term of office, they frequently become less active in the church and sometimes drop out altogether. Clearly those responsible for church administration need to develop a new approach to meetings. Pastors are failing to take advantage of the opportunities present to assist people in their spiritual growth.

Pastors can influence change in this situation by viewing each meeting as an occasion for spiritual growth. Creating opportunities for growth in the context of meetings requires a change in procedure. Clergy can allow time for the sharing of personal stories. Through this sharing, people learn to know and trust one another. Pastors can begin meetings by paying attention to the needs of those present so those persons can release things that might otherwise disrupt or subvert the meeting. Such a check-in time can break down walls of isolation and affirm each member as valued.

A second way of introducing change into the meeting is to have an extended time of prayer, not just the formal opening prayer. A bidding prayer in which the leader invites all present to share joys, sorrows, and concerns opens the door to include everyone. The leader allows plenty of time after the first prayers spoken to encourage shyer members to express their concerns. Shared prayer also signals the meeting's spiritual nature.

Several church boards meet on alternate months for business. The leadership shapes the nonbusiness meetings around personal concerns, sharing of ideas, telling faith stories, prayer, and Bible study. The common discovery of the groups that have tried this plan is that they get as much business accomplished as they previously did, and people generally feel better about themselves and one another. Members look forward to being together and even the business meetings have a more personal feel, as if the presence of each person was a real gift that mattered to the whole group.

Changing the focus of meetings from agenda to discerning God's work in the group is a major shift. One of the tools at the disposal of the pastor attempting to make this shift is the practice of group spiritual direction. Group spiritual direction assists members in noticing God's action in their individual lives as well as in the community setting. Group spiritual direction seeks to help the group pay attention to God, deepen its collective prayer forms, and respond to God's invitation to fulfill the divine calling in their particular structure.

One way to conceive of an agenda for a business meeting for spiritual growth might look something like a spiritual direction session:

Greeting
    The words to part of a psalm

A time of silence
A time of check-in

Prayer
Shared prayer for one another
Approval of the minutes and the agenda
Singing of a hymn

Presentation of Issues
The telling of one life-story
Presentation of major reports
Time of sharing of scripture or some spiritual discipline

Assessment
Discussion and action on the items of business
A time of silence
Reflection on needed follow-up to actions taken
A time of prayer for the congregation
Planning for the next meeting
Sharing gifts: What each takes away from the meeting

Departure
Singing of a hymn or repeating a psalm
Benediction

Such an order of business differs greatly from the usual agenda for a business meeting. The leaders might use the structure of a worship service with each part of the service—from Greeting to Benediction—represented in the agenda. They should attempt to place the agenda within a structure that emphasizes the group's spiritual development rather than business. Sometimes pressing business issues will require the abbreviation of other aspects. However, their presence, even in shortened form, will still make a difference in the way business is acted upon.

Group spiritual direction and guidance has some limitations:

1. It is easier to hide in a group than in one-to-one situations. People can sit back rather than speak. Others may interpret their silence as politeness when, in fact, it is evasion or avoidance.

2. A few strong, outgoing individuals may dominate the group and exclude those less able to assert themselves. The leader will attempt to maintain a balance so that those least likely to speak out get an opportunity to do so.

3. Group members may use agenda items to prevent the group from attending to the spiritual issues present. Most small groups have more than one purpose. Unless designed for spiritual direction alone, every other agenda item may distract from paying attention.

Sometimes pastors may use the small group as a vehicle for spiritual direction; other times trying to change the purpose of an existing group may be unwise. A discerning leader will recognize the appropriate time to refer a person to a specialized group or to a personal spiritual director. People who are going through a period of great awakening or dryness may need group involvement that allows them to view their own experience in light of others' experiences. Whenever we can see ourselves in perspective through the experience of others, we may obtain a much needed look at ourselves. We also discover that we are not alone in our struggles or joys. Whatever we're feeling within ourselves, shared experiences can sustain us in dry times and keep us on course in times of great enthusiasm.

Group spiritual direction is important for every congregation because no pastor can offer individual direction to all the members, even those who seek it. Even when the pastor concentrates upon a small group of leaders who then become spiritual directors for others, thereby increasing the opportunities for spiritual growth within the congregation, the demand to direct a great many people is hard to meet. Most members of a congregation either will receive group direction or they will get none at all.

Pastors must seek and pursue opportunities for spiritual growth in every small group within the congregation. The pastor's own involvement in small groups will lead to an understanding of how to facilitate such groups successfully. Each small group is a potential source for spiritual growth. Every committee and board presents a pastoral challenge to create space for spiritual renewal in the midst of doing business. Such spiritual guidance offers the church the possibility of moving beyond business as usual.

CHAPTER NINE

The Pastor as Person: Keeping Our Souls Alive

I WANT TO UNDERSCORE the danger of the pastoral vocation. I fear this chapter may sound like bad news, but I believe we can bring healing to our vocation by naming the powers and principalities that may come to distract us from our calling. The number of disciplinary charges filed against ministers within every denomination and the lawsuits filed against churches by people who protest that their pastor has harmed them make us wonder what is wrong. I know from my twenty-nine years of experience of teaching and counseling seminary students that pastors are people who set out to do good. They enter seminary with high ideals and a sense of personal call from God. I have been forced to wonder what has caused these otherwise idealistic people to compromise their dreams and betray their high calling. These compromises and betrayals point to the changing tenor of the times and to the toll that the practice of ministry takes on pastors.

Sometimes the profession of ministry has not strengthened the faith of those called to this vocation. The pastoral vocation has caused them to become immune to the very gospel they have proclaimed. Words such as *gospel, forgiveness,* and *new life* may seem to apply only to parishioners and not to pastors themselves. The tragic experience of many clergy is common enough to cause every pastor to wonder, *Am I immune from the disease that ravages so many of my peers?*

THE PROBLEMS CLERGY FACE

Many pastors speak about the difficulty they have in their personal worship of God. Pastors lead worship yet we ourselves have trouble worshiping. Activities such as prayer and meditative reading of scripture may have become tools of the trade to the extent that these spiritual disciplines no longer nourish the souls of pastors. Pastors may find themselves going through the motions of the faith, talking about it a great deal but unsure of their actual beliefs. Cheapening the sacred is hard to avoid if what we commend to others is not a source of awe in our personal lives. One of the gravest problems of the practice of ministry today is the inability of pastors to receive sustenance from the practices normative for other Christians.

All pastors need to make some provision for their own need for worship. Attending a church of another denomination that differs greatly from one's own arouses the critical faculties less because we have less information and experience, and we are much less likely to criticize what is new and different. Protestant clergy who attend a service of monastic hours in a community of religious sisters or brothers discover that the service differs enough to require learning afresh, and the times of services are such that a pastor's schedule can accommodate them.

Pastoral ministry takes a great deal out of its practitioners. Clergy who have served as long-time parish ministers often say that ministry is no longer fun. Church infighting seems to grow increasingly frequent and increasingly venomous. Many congregations today are places of considerable conflict. Often pastors are drawn into the heart of the conflict and blamed by all sides for what is wrong. The stress level for pastors is high; the price of keeping warring parties at peace takes a great deal of energy. Pastors also deal with deeply troubled people on a regular basis. Clergy are the first line of approach for people who are unwilling or unable to deal with mental health professionals, either because they cannot afford the cost or because they fear the consequences of getting tangled in the system. Thus at every level, institutional and personal, pastors find themselves involved in high-stress activity.

Congregations today expect the pastor to move beyond the traditional tasks of preaching, conducting worship, and providing pastoral care for the sick and grieving. Parishioners expect the pastor to be a conflict manager, an evangelist who can attract new members—especially young, affluent ones—and someone who can manage both the spiritual and the temporal affairs of the congregation, all the while preaching inspiring sermons and paying close attention to the personal needs of the membership.

Added to this job description is our society's growing discontent with any form of authority and every authority figure. Pastors represent the authority of God and are therefore the object of considerable resentment. People's anger at the IRS or the government or the community zoning commission or the price of gasoline often vents itself in anticlericalism. People cannot easily or effectively express their anger. Then this bottled-up anger gets dumped on the one accessible authority figure. The less personal power people have in their own lives, the more angry and resentful they are likely to be. In the pastor, their resentment finds a ready target for expression.

In most congregations, whatever the denomination's polity, members may try to get rid of the pastor with careful planning, skillful organization, and hard work. A few dedicated laypersons seem to specialize in the practice of destroying pastors. These persons, whom G. Lloyd Rediger has called "clergy killers," operate with effectiveness in many congregations. "Clergy killers typically have intimidating power because they are willing to violate the rules of decorum and caring the rest of us try to follow. This is powerful at a subconscious level, for we sense such persons are willing to escalate the fight and use tactics we forbid to use ourselves."[1] Their success increases their appetite for more. Their activity is not fully conscious; people who engage in pastor bashing may do so for reasons beyond their understanding. What they know is that the pastor has disappointed them. The pastor is lazy or incompetent. The pastor is power hungry or irresponsible. The pastor plays favorites, or the pastor is aloof. The pastor is disorganized, or the pastor is rigid. In short, the pastor cannot satisfy them.

Encounters with these "clergy killers" make a pastor suspicious and bitter. Both suspicion and bitterness are spiritual illnesses that damage the spirit. Deeply hurt pastors become brittle, and the practice of ministry destroys them. Damaged spirits become disillusioned and cynical about the high ideals that existed at the start of their pastoral ministries. Damaged spirits may seek revenge against those who have hurt them or against parishioners in general. Cynicism among clergy may cause them to take advantage of those parishioners who come to them in trust.

In addition to neglecting our spiritual health, pastors may neglect or mistreat our bodies as a result of the stress involved in dealing with high levels of conflict. We may ignore our body's signals for needed rest. We may drive ourselves until the signs of stress appear as one of several serious illnesses. At heart, the problem of pastoral ministry is a spiritual problem. Every pastor needs to be prepared for bad days when defenses are down, when faith may seem like a foolish dream, when life is deeply disappointing. Every pastor needs to live in such a way that nurtures faith as food for the soul. Every pastor needs to put on the whole armor of God as a shield against the spiritual poisons of bitterness, cynicism, despair, self-doubt, and faith-lessness.

SOURCES OF HELP AND SUPPORT

Regular spiritual practices protect people from the tendency to exhaust themselves and to deplete their spiritual resources. For pastors, these practices may help us guard against burnout with its loss of energy. Some pastors evidence burnout by going through the motions without any passion. They have been emptied of inspiration by ideals that have been compromised and wonderful plans that have been shot down by congregations unwilling to change. Regular attention to the care of our own souls is not optional for pastors; it may be the only way we can continue the practice of ministry without losing our souls in the process.

Every pastor needs someone who can act as a mentor or wise guide. The work of ministry is too dangerous to attempt by oneself. Our highly valued individualism has come back to haunt us; the price we pay for our freedom is loneliness and isolation. Many pastors have no one to whom they can turn for advice, correction, or encouragement. They do not dare speak of their most intimate needs and desires with those within the congregation for fear of destroying the pastoral relationship. They also may not speak from the heart with those in authority in their denominational structure for fear that they will be thought less of or passed up for promotions. They may not trust their colleagues in ministry out of a desire to look respectable or strong for the sake of the congregation they serve. Their spouses cannot bear the full weight of responsibility for mentoring them.

Those of us whose lives have lost a sense of the holy because we talk about holy things all the time may need a neutral person to help point the way to an ongoing discovery of God's presence in our lives. The spiritual guide may require a guide. Most pastors need to find a spiritual director who will help us stay spiritually alive. The director can assist the pastor in dealing with issues of faith and doubt, with matters of stress and bitterness. The spiritual director may be the one person who can help the pastor keep faith alive in the darkest of days. Above all, the spiritual director is someone to whom the pastor can be accountable. Just knowing that we are accountable for our thoughts and actions may prevent habits of bitterness and cynicism from becoming ingrained.

Therapists also serve as valuable persons in the lives of pastors. The therapist may be the one person to whom the pastor would dare to tell the full truth about himself or herself. But unless the therapist is a person of faith, he or she may be ill-equipped to assist pastors with issues of faith and doubt and personal issues such as sexuality, power, authority, and competition. Along with a therapist, a spiritual director can help the pastor work on issues that have to do with personal faith issues: questions related to a sense of God's call, a sense of God's continuing presence, the practice of prayer, strengthening the inner life to resist the power of cynicism.

Many pastors have a difficult time finding anyone to whom we can turn on a regular basis. Our lack of a confidant often gets us into trouble. Left to our own devices, we are unable to recognize our own wounds, much less heal them. We may be our own worst counselor, yet that is what a great many pastors try to do. Because we are able to help other persons, we believe we need no one's help. We may even believe that seeking help indicates a lack of faith. We keep striving until we break under the load.

Pastors isolated geographically from sources of help may have to create their own helping relationships through the use of e-mail or the telephone. It might be possible to form a small group of pastors or other professionals in the community who are able to be honest with one another, who can keep confidences, and who are relatively free from the need to be better than their peers. This support group may provide a significant source of spiritual strength for the members so long as they work together for a period of time to build the necessary trust.

SELF-EXAMINATION AND SELF-KNOWLEDGE

In addition to these relationships, pastors must accept responsibility for maintaining our own faith as a personal discipline. Pastors cannot avoid the effort that personal discipline entails, although it appears to be more difficult for some than for others and certainly the methods of sustaining personal discipline vary from person to person. With the help of trusted others, we can come to see ourselves honestly and discover both our strengths and potential weaknesses.

Being aware of how we grow and become our best self is important; only then may we practice those disciplines that will be most beneficial. For example, if we need time alone to recharge after expending ourselves for others, then we may need to set a regular schedule of retreat—as frequently as one afternoon a week or at least one day a month—to go away to a retreat center or place of refuge for quiet and solitude. The time set aside is time with God, soul time, sacred time. Without silence, many people will feel drained of spiritual energy quickly. Other people may find such periods of time burdensome; they may need to take time out occasionally, but retreat is not the primary means of their spiritual growth. These pastors grow most from a clergy lectionary study group where they can exchange ideas, pray together, and be inspired by others. Still others may grow by spending time out-of-doors in the garden, hiking, biking, rock climbing or some other activity.

Establishing our priorities requires a degree of self-awareness. Attempting to force ourselves into the use of an inappropriate discipline or one that does not encourage our fullest growth may cause harm.

In the same way, knowing our weaknesses and thus the source of our greatest temptation is very important. This knowledge enables us to protect ourselves from some subtle temptations. Temptations are likely to come from unmet needs, unhealed wounds, unresolved doubts, and lack of clarity around certain issues. Self-understanding is critical for any form of discernment about right and wrong. We learn at least as much from our weaknesses as from our strengths.

If, for example, our weak spot is the need for approval from others because we received infrequent parental approval, our greatest temptation to compromise principles may come in our efforts to gain that approval. We may learn the terrible truth that we will do almost anything to get a compliment, including breaking confidences or lying.

Our weakness may be a poor self-image. The wound is caused by the failure to honor or cherish our unique self before God. We do not really believe our own spoken words about forgiveness and new life. We may feel these words apply to others but not to us personally. We need other people to prop us up. If this is our weakness, we are vulnerable to criticism because we will tend to believe almost anything negative that others say. Many pastors remain almost incapable of hearing praise while even a hint of criticism will plunge them into deep depression. Because the pastoral ministry is often the object of criticism, any pastors who cannot handle criticism may spend much time in depression and doubt about whether their call is really from God. Each weak spot leads to its own destructive end.

Both forms of self-knowledge—knowing what nourishes and what tempts—are important. By knowing these, we can engage in those activities that enliven and enhance our ministry, while avoiding those things that destroy and tear down.

Within some limits, pastors may shift priorities in ways that produce maximum personal satisfaction. Often we spend too much time engaged in draining activities to the neglect of those activities that energize. Only those activities that feed the soul will keep us alive spiritually.

Pastors might consider negotiating with the Personnel Committee or the Pastor-Parish Relations Committee to discuss ways of enhancing our particular strengths. If reading and reflection time nourishes us, we might interpret that fact to the congregation and its officers. Such activity is not an escape from work unless taken to an extreme; rather it is a way of keeping ourselves alive so that other pastoral work will benefit. Sometimes pastors use study time as an excuse to avoid dealing with people, but most clergy would benefit from more study time. The goal is finding a proper balance in life. Those who live from their strengths are happy people. Happy pastors can give of themselves without becoming bitter or burning out.

SPIRITUAL DISCIPLINES

1 One helpful spiritual discipline is *keeping a journal.* Writing down our thoughts on a regular basis enables us to look at repetitive life themes. If we discover ourselves in the midst of a dark time when God seems distant and work is painfully hard, looking back in the pages of a journal to other such periods may prove helpful. We may discover patterns, such as a particular time of year or level of pastoral activity that causes the down time. While we cannot avoid celebrating Christmas, the memory of painful childhood Christmases may be the source of great sorrow at a time of year when others seem to be happy; this knowledge may help us get through the darkness of such a time.

Journaling also allows us to look back and see the times when faith seemed most real, prayer life vital, and ministry most fulfilling. Such times offer blessing and strength in the dark times. No one lives on the mountaintop all the time, but rereading journal entries can significantly impact our sense of balance. The journal reminds us of the pattern of ups and downs present in every life.

2 Another helpful spiritual discipline is that of maintaining a *balance between work and play.* When we discover delight in play, whether in competitive sports or in a solitary activity like tending a flower bed or some art or craft, we have found a key to avoiding self-absorption in work. Many pastors make the mistake of equating being busy with being faithful. No such correlation exists. Being busy may be a way of avoiding a situation that needs attention. Playful activity can renew us, recharge our souls, and make us better pastors. Of course, finding the time for play may force us to say no to some other activity.

3 *Self-care* is a spiritual discipline exercised by saying no. For some people saying no seems like an act of betrayal of the Lord. Instead, such an act may signal our willingness to engage in self-care. Another form of self-care involves taking care of our body. Cherishing our body can be a form of spiritual discipline. Our body is a gift from God. Engaging in activity that destroys one's body results in failure to appreciate the gift. Nutritious diet, exercise, and adequate rest: All are ways we care for our body. There is a direct relationship between care for the body and care for the soul.

4 *Prayer* bears close relationship to the body. Fatigue or sluggishness from overeating prevents us from praying well. Prayer is the heart of the Christian life. We need to keep that discipline alive in an appropriate form. All clergy will discover prayer as a private discipline, but the form may differ from one to another. Some pastors will discover the joy of centering, wordless prayer. Others will benefit most from following a prayer book, reading the great prayers of others as an aid to personal prayer. Still others will use pictures, icons, or other objects as a means to bring about a sense of God's presence. We also benefit from small prayer groups in which we can pray aloud without worrying about what parishioners may think.

Prayer is an exercise of faith. Every time we pray, we are acting upon faith in a living, caring God. In prayer we assume the presence of God to whom we turn for help for ourselves and those we love. Our prayers are, in themselves, aids to faith. Most pastors find themselves engaged in the practice of intercessory prayer on a regular basis. In our desire to assist others, we need not neglect prayers for ourselves and our families.

168 ~~ CHAPTER NINE

5 High on my list of spiritual disciplines is the *sacrament of Holy Communion*. For many Christians of all denominations, Communion is central for spirituality. How can pastors receive nurture from the Lord's Supper and serve as celebrants also? We may find ourselves so caught up in the particulars of presiding and our concern for a smoothly run service that we do not receive the spiritual benefits of the sacrament. Pastors may receive nurture from the Lord's Supper in two ways. One, we benefit from frequent celebration. If we celebrate often enough, it becomes a part of us and our worries about doing it "right" or making some mistake become minimal. Our goal becomes sharing in the experience along with the other participants. Two, every pastor will benefit from occasions to receive the sacrament when another pastor is the celebrant. Such occasions may include meetings of conferences, presbyteries, or associations. Denominational executives also may include those times when pastors can attend a service of Holy Communion at another church in the community.

6 The other primary discipline for the spiritual life is the *reading of scripture*. The Bible is an important source of strength only if we use it for more than potential sermon material. All pastors need to discover the Bible as a book that nourishes. If the Bible can become an instrument for our encounter with the living God, then we will grow from reading it. However, if while we read the Bible we are thinking about a sermon or class the Bible will have only utilitarian value. Every pastor needs to recover a reflective/meditative approach to scripture like that practiced for centuries. Such a meditative method of reading scripture leads one to ascertain the feel of the text. Then the focus becomes the encounter between the reader and the text. The purpose of this method is not to learn more but to meet the living God.

Spiritual disciplines allow clergy to exercise responsible self-love. Self-love, rather than being a sign of selfishness, is a sign that we take seriously the need to cultivate our most fully developed self as an instrument to serve God. We must sustain that self at its best in order to serve most helpfully. Miserable people who are duty bound but joyless are not likely to lead anyone else to an appreciation of the gospel. As we cherish the gift that makes each human being unique and special, we will discover that taking care of self is an act of faithfulness to God.

All persons engaged in a helping profession need some kind of discipline to keep going. The action of helping others can be draining and exhausting if we have no ways to renew our inner strength. The disciplines equip persons for more effective ministry by helping us become healthier persons. Not all disciplines are practiced easily, and some of us resist them because they do not seem to fit our personality. Such resistance may be an important clue to the "wrongness" of a particular discipline for us. On the other hand, we may feel uncomfortable for a while until the discipline becomes habitual. Some disciplines take time in order to touch our hearts and enable us to grow more fully into the persons God intends us to be. We may find it difficult to discern whether our struggle with a given discipline is a sign to let it go or to keep trying. A spiritual director or guide can assist in such discernment.

Whatever the shape of our own spiritual lives, the task of keeping our souls alive is the single most important activity in which pastors can engage. Without stretching our souls, we can dry up and become immune to the words and acts that form the heart of our pastoral work. We may end up cynical and bitter even as we preach faith and hope. Setting our own spiritual growth as a high priority is not selfishness. When we are growing in faith, we are at our best for others.

CHAPTER TEN

Spirituality as the Authority for Pastoral Ministry

T HE ISSUE OF AUTHORITY remains central to the work of pastoral ministry. Authority provides the power to function in a given situation. Because authority has to do with power, we cannot ignore issues of authority, such as who has authority, how it is given or taken, how it is exercised. The answers to such issues bear a strong relation to our satisfaction in pastoral ministry, and we cannot divorce authority in the church from authority in the culture at large.

Authority is the power or right to influence the actions of others. Authority is closely related to authorization; to exercise authority is to receive the right to power from a higher source By itself, authority is a neutral power that one can exercise for good or evil. That authority may be legal or moral; it may be the authority of office or the authority of personality. Authority comes in different forms, but all have to do with the same questions: Can I do what needs to be done? Do I have sufficient power to accomplish necessary tasks? Who authorizes me to perform my work? To whom am I accountable for my work?

We live in a time when authority is suspect; it is a time of massive disillusionment about far-off decision makers who affect the direction of our lives. Deep resentment is aimed at most institutions and professions: organized medicine and medical doctors, organized government and politicians, organized law and lawyers, organized religion and ministers. People have a hard time expressing their resentment toward many of these professionals; they feel relatively helpless. That feeling of powerlessness may surface most clearly in the one remaining place where people can still participate in the decision making, and that is the church. Here is the place where the average citizen can still exercise some authority—even over the pastor. People may take out some of their frustration with authority by acting against ecclesiastical authority. We see signs of this rebellion in the attitudes of many people toward denominational leadership. The further from the local church that the decisions are made, the more suspect this distant authority becomes. People may vent this anger at the pastor's authority.

Even as persons seek out pastors for clues about the nature of the divine/human encounter, others resist the pastors and resent their authority. This double message is a constant fact of ministry. People appear to give out two conflicting messages. The first message may be, "We want you to be more authoritative and to give clearer leadership. Tell us what you want, what your dreams are so we will be able to follow. We want you to be a strong leader." The second message is, "You are a dictator, and you try to get your own way too much. Your ways are authoritarian and demanding. Give us a chance to express our ideas and share in the decision making. It is our church too." This love/hate relationship with parishioners can produce different pastoral responses.

Parishioners' unexamined ambivalence often makes pastors

the object of intense feelings. A pastor has the power to hurt others deeply and to discourage people. The heart of the authority for pastoral ministry resides in the awesome power that ministers possess, whether we admit it or not. The potential power and actual power of the pastor may be particularly dangerous. If I do not recognize my own power, I may take subtle advantage of those I am to serve. I may hurt people without feeling much guilt if they threaten or attack me, and I see them as potential enemies. Pastors who feel helpless or devoid of power can do serious harm in their efforts to prove their power.

FORMS OF AUTHORITY

In every significant human relationship, power and authority exist in some form. One person usually has more authority than the other, as in the relationship of parent and child, teacher and student, doctor and patient, or pastor and parishioner. The power behind the particular authority may lie in the power of personality, age, education, position, or charm. One may give away power to another because of a need for approval, or the person who wants to have his or her own way may demand it. Authority takes at least four different forms. Persons may exercise each when conditions permit. Each form may fit a particular relationship.

1 *The first form of authority is the authority of law.* We generally connect this legal form of authority with the power to punish those who disobey. The formal authority of the police or the Internal Revenue Service belongs in this category. At one time the church had the full authority of law, and pastors exercised the power of the state, such as in colonial New England. Pastors have not had this kind of authority since the disestablishment of the churches of Europe and America.

Legal authority is not present; no power of the state enforces the moral or religious authority of any pastor.

Pastors do express legal authority today in the relationship between employer and employee. Authority rests in the power of the employer to terminate the employment of the employee. Authority takes the form of the command, "Do what I say, or there will be negative consequences." Pastors have a limited form of this authority over members of the church staff, but even then this power is usually modified by the church governing body or church council that has final authority over terms of employment.

2 *The second form of authority is the authority of office.* The President of the United States has certain authority by virtue of office. Pastors have this kind of authority also. We have the authority to celebrate the sacraments, to preach, and to preside at certain governing body meetings. Although this form of authority may carry little direct power, the office of pastor carries great potential power. The authority of preaching gives every pastor a certain kind of moral power in the congregation. Week after week, people come to hear what the pastor will say. They generally trust that the pastor's words are reliable, so they take those words seriously. Few people in our society have such a ready-made audience eager to hear their ideas with so much attentiveness. The office of pastor carries with it the authority to speak for God, to represent divine authority. This is an awesome authority.

Every pastor needs to be aware of the power that comes with the pastoral office. The ordaining body bestows that power; the people who look to the pastor for guidance in their lives accept that power. They will acknowledge pastoral authority vested in the office, for which they generally have high respect.

A gender difference operates here. Parishioners are not likely to give women pastors the authority of office because they still do not feel completely at ease with the presence of women clergy. Women clergy may need to claim their authority more directly than men. Wearing a pulpit robe is one way the woman pastor demonstrates the authority of her office, while for a male pastor, taking off the robe is a way of being just "one of the guys" and may win praise.

3 *The third form of authority is the authority of persuasion.* All pastors have the authority of persuasion, which is given to us in ordination. We can use the pulpit to persuade, but we have other avenues for the exercise of this form of authority. We can persuade through our teaching, through our leadership of church boards, and through our one–to–one pastoral care situations. We can use the power of persuasion in every situation where people give us a hearing. Skilled pastors can persuade people to follow them, accept their ideas, and trust them.

Sometimes pastors have more success in this enterprise than is good for them or their parishioners. The abuse of the power of persuasion is more subtle than most other forms of pastoral abuse; it happens when persuasion becomes a battle of wills. Sometimes pastors win a victory but actually lose because in the process we have had our own way at the expense of other people. People who lose the battle prepare better the next time. They come to the battle ready to claim their own power. The next time the pastor tries to get something done, the people are more suspicious, more likely to resist; they dig in their heels. The next time conflict arises, the pastor may suffer a serious loss and then will come a visit from those in authority asking for termination of the pastoral relationship.

Pastors can and do misuse the authority of persuasion. Sometimes we become overly confident in our own truth: We are tempted to "play God" with our words, and we come to believe that we know what is best for everyone else. Such egotism and abuse of this pastoral authority produces two very different results. One is the rise in anticlericalism from those who resent being told how to behave in the world by someone who seems to believe the answers are obvious. Some pastors have been guilty of claiming to know the answer to every question. People sitting in the pew value their own knowledge of the world; they want to trust their experience of life while affirming that their education and training have prepared them for appropriate and intelligent decision making. They do not appreciate the efforts of anyone, including the pastor, to control or dominate them. Efforts that tell them what to do fail to appreciate their value or worth and demean their ethical ability.

A second result is that some pastors have sought to exercise the authority of persuasion for ourselves by distancing ourselves from the people. Through our education and ordination we have sought to create as much mystery about ourselves as possible, perhaps referring to ourselves (usually with the first person plural) in sermons as illustrations of faithful response to the gospel. We may even adapt a pious tone to our speech that calls attention to our personal holiness. Such pastors can make people feel somewhat guilty for existing and apologetic about their own lives. Yet because we fulfill parishioners' deep-seated expectations, we are often held in high esteem, praised by our people, and well rewarded financially. The problem occurs when we are unable to carry out this mysterious sense of holiness forever. If and when we show our humanity in even the mildest of departures from expectation, we find ourselves in deep trouble. Because we have claimed to be more than human, the exposure of our humanity is all the more shocking. The authority claimed by these pastors is the authority of position and role, an authority that often is welcomed but is difficult to follow up. This authority expresses itself in words such as, "Do what I say; after all, I am the pastor." To rely on office for authority is not new or unique, but it is dangerous if office is the *only* basis for that authority.

Church members will accept persuasive authority eagerly. In a confusing world of too many choices, people hunger for an authority that speaks directly and commandingly. People want some clues to guide them through the maze of moral confusion and diversity of style of life that exists everywhere in our culture. They seek someone who has special access to and possession of moral and religious qualities that they lack. Pastors who tell them what to think, to feel, and to do attract these needy persons. Such pastoral authority allows them to cease the struggle to find their own way. It is easy to obey another person so long as one can believe that the other person has a direct word from God. The appeal of religious authoritarianism is one reason pastors who offer answers and demand obedience are often quite successful. Many people respond positively, at least for a while, to the exercise of direct religious authority. This kind of authority often falls victim to demagoguery.

4 *The fourth form of authority is the authority of the person.* Pastors have authority because we are trustworthy people. Our consistency in leadership has merited congregational trust. Parishioners see in us a sincerity and integrity that have great appeal in a society that tends to demean leadership. The pastor's personal authority does not come about overnight. Pastors have to work over a period of years to get this

kind of authority. Personal authority does not, in fact, come about by working hard to get it. Personal authority is a gift others bestow; we can never demand or coerce it. Personal authority comes as a gift through our faithfulness to the various duties of pastoral ministry. A pastor who calls upon parishioners regularly, attends to their spiritual needs, is compassionate and caring, faithfully interprets the Word of God week after week, and does not violate trust acquires this kind of authority without seeking it or even knowing it is there.

Another gender difference: Women pastors arouse less suspicion and open hostility than do their male counterparts. People are more likely to trust women, in part, because they have no prior experience with female leaders. Women leaders have not betrayed them. Not knowing what it is to have a woman leader who tries to manipulate or control them, parishioners may be more ready to grant personal authority to the woman pastor.

Congregational members expect pastors, whether male or female, to be more learned about the faith than other people. Parishioners also expect pastors to model that faith, bearing witness to an intimate and authoritative relationship with God. Pastors' prayer lives serve as a standard for others. What the people seek above all is integrity. They want their pastors to live out what they proclaim from the pulpit, to be consistent with the message they preach and teach. They want to see what Christianity looks like when taken seriously. They want the pastor to show them that the Christian life is possible.

To serve as a congregational example is, by definition, to be somewhat different. What pastors make of the difference, which comes by virtue of calling and ordination, is crucial. The difference can be a shield pastors employ to hide from genuine relationships with other people. The difference may force pastors to conform to popular conventions and prevailing habits of a group of people held captive to whatever parochial definitions of the"good life" are operative in a particular congregation. The difference may grow out of the pastor's own integrity. As we seek to be true to our own faith, to the high calling of Christ, to our own gifts, and to the maintenance of the spiritual life as a priority, a difference may express itself. This difference is not capitulation to expectations or the exaggeration of a role; this difference is formed by faithfulness, which is worthy of emulation.

The difference in a pastor's life reflects intensity in the venture of faith, a challenge to the spiritual lethargy that keeps the church in bondage to its culture. This difference springs from the position of pastor as one who dares to be a person for others. Pastors who live into this difference gladly accept the uniqueness of the pastoral role and seek to live it with integrity. For that reason, a pastor will "put one's own search for God with all the moments of pain and joy, despair and hope, at the disposal of those who want to join the search but do not know how." Pastors with this kind of integrity speak truth to the people, using ordinary language that has meaning in the people's own experience. These clergy refuse to trivialize language by falling back into trite expressions that have lost meaning. The authority claimed here is the authority of the person. The danger rests in the pastor's failure to be honest, in which case the lack of integrity will unmask whatever fragile authority exists.

TO CONSIDER OUR OWN CALLING is to recognize that authority does not come from ourselves but from God. Pastoral authority stems from God's grace. God's call into ministry is itself a bestowal of authority. Denominational structures demonstrate their own acknowledgement of that divine authority.

They do this throughout the process of guidance, culminating in the act of ordination. Ordination is the church's action to validate and authorize a person to engage in ministry. At ordination, the ordinand receives the power to perform various actions not otherwise permitted. The authority to preach, to baptize, and to celebrate Holy Communion are often unique responsibilities of those who are ordained.

We can move in several directions in our efforts to find an authority appropriate to ourselves and our congregations:

First, we can *attempt to disavow authority*. Some ministers fear authority and pretend they have none. This strategy sounds appealing; these pastors seem so egalitarian and humble that people actually want to believe that the pastor has no desire to exercise power. The danger is that no one, including the pastor, is aware of the actual authority that is present. Denying authority may make people happy, but authority does not go away. A certain dishonesty about this pretense, of which the pastor may be unaware, may become obvious to other people. They recognize that only the pastor has the power to reach the congregation every Sunday. Access to the pulpit differentiates the power of the pastor from that of church members. Pastors have more authority than they know.

A second direction is to *claim authority at all costs* and become dominating dictators. Few of us think of ourselves in such negative terms. Most often, we believe we should deny our authority in an attempt to seem more Christlike. The hollowness of such a pretense becomes clear when some issue presents itself, and we suddenly demand a particular response. Without warning we move from the egalitarian claim of having no authority to an insistence on having our own way. With no preparation for the apparent change of heart, parishioners are surprised, hurt, and angry. We seem to have betrayed our own words about there being no inequality of power among the people. Yet pastors possess authority even when not exercising it.

A third direction is to *share authority with others*. Shared authority remains authority while avoiding the "we/they" character of personal or official authority. When we feel strong enough, we can let go of our need to be right and to have our own way; we respect the wisdom of the elected congregational leaders. These hard-working volunteers bring wisdom about the church and experience in the community that we may lack. Listening and heeding their wisdom endows them with authority, which empowers them to do their best.

The real issue is the purpose for the authority. One may have authority over another; such authority is the power to control or dominate another person. This kind of authority nearly always feels unpleasant; we tend to resist such authority as a way of maintaining our personal freedom. Mark's Gospel exemplifies the authority of the scribes and the Pharisees in this way. The religious rulers of Jesus' day used their office to control other people. Other religious leaders have attempted to use their authority in like manners. We almost instinctively resent efforts to take away our own power. Authority over another feels invasive to the other person, and it frequently threatens people. They feel demeaned by the effort to dominate them.

THE ESSENCE OF AUTHORITY FOR MINISTRY

Another form of authority is that of *service*. This is authority exercised on behalf of another. Jesus exercised such authority, and the people recognized it: "They were astounded at his teaching, for he taught them as one having authority" (Mark 1:22). Jesus exercised his authority on behalf of those he came to serve and save. He sought to use his power to assist rather than to control those he encountered. He taught them as one who cared about their well-being. He wanted them to experience their God-given freedom and wholeness; he had no interest in forcing them into particular behaviors. Jesus sought free response from others because of his care for them.

Our resistance to our own possible source of authority may signal misunderstanding about the nature of our calling. We quite properly resist authority as domination and control, as authority over others. We as pastors need a sense of authority on behalf of people. Jesus challenged the status quo in his day through a series of words and actions aimed at the usual understanding of authority and power. Illustrations of the overturn of power and authority fill his life: his choice of women and Samaritans, sinners and outcasts, invalids and "nobodies" as friends and disciples; his entrance into Jerusalem on a donkey; his death as a common criminal. All of these events dramatically signal Jesus' rejection of the normally accepted structure of authority and power.

Children are central to Jesus' teaching about power and authority. In Luke we read,

> People were bringing even infants to him that he might touch them; and when the disciples saw it, they sternly ordered them not to do it. But Jesus called for them and said, "Let the little children come to me, and do not stop them; for it is to such as these that the kingdom of God belongs. Truly I tell you, whoever does not receive the kingdom of God as a little child will never enter it" (Luke 18:15-17).

Children are people without power. Jesus' use of them to model life in the reign of God is significant: His followers are to understand authority as mutuality. If Jesus sets children before us as our examples, then we must accept the surrender of power that comes with being disciples of the one who gave up power in order to be faithful to God.

> Let the same mind be in you that was in Christ Jesus,
> who, though he was in the form of God,
> did not regard equality with God
> as something to be exploited,
> but emptied himself,
> taking the form of a slave,
> being born in human likeness.
> And being found in human form,
> he humbled himself
> and became obedient to the point of death—
> even death on a cross (Phil. 2:5-8).

The emptying of self is a difficult task. Deeply ingrained within us all is the connection between power and self-worth. We feel that we have value to the extent that we are able to exercise control over others; when we have no control, we feel worthless. We become fearful, and we worry that others may take advantage of us. Our struggle to get and use power over others represents an almost desperate effort to hang on to our sense of importance. The ability to surrender power may require God's help.

God in Christ is not the God of power and control but the God who puts aside power to be available to us and with us. Christ is God, laying aside power and becoming weak, helpless, and vulnerable. Jesus girded himself with a towel and got down on his knees to wash his disciples' feet, reversing the order of power for all time. This God invites us into relationship as partners—not to submit ourselves to arbitrary authority but to accept responsibility for the power we do possess. God becomes a partner with us rather than a controller, thus enabling us to partner with those around us.

Ridding ourselves of our controlling image of God as almighty and dominating, and raising up the image of God as one who lays aside power for the benefit of us all, enables us to see that getting and keeping power is not the goal of life. We then may begin the process of living in relationship with God as friend and companion. We discover the gentle love of this God who is not an arbitrary despot, and we may then discover our own gentleness with other people. If the nature of reality is not a pyramid with one person at the top and the rest arranged in subservient roles below, a new reality can empower us to act differently.

To trust God is to believe that God does not ask us to engage in self-destruction. Because God longs for relationship, the love of God is always directed toward the good of people. God's grace is never destructive because God always wills our best. Even though we sense the danger inherent in discipleship, our ability to trust in God's love enables us to accept the call of God. In the call, God may ask us to let go of something dear or to shed some pattern of behavior that has become a bad habit or source of distraction; but God's ultimate goal is for healing and shaping us more fully into the people God intends that we become.

MUTUALITY IN THE BODY OF CHRIST

Our attitude toward power—our appreciation of its dangers and our respect for its value—call for a transformation of the self. We need to be changed.

- First, we need to discover that we matter ultimately to God and that we do not have to prove our worth to God or to ourselves. The security of knowing our worth is the beginning of our ability to give away power.

- Second, we need to find positive ways to use power on behalf of others. We often persuade ourselves that we know what is best for others and thus have a duty to win them over to our point of view. We have to be sure that our motive really is the enhancement, not diminution, of another's strengths. Because we have power in many different situations, what we do with our power is important.

- Third, we need to learn a new way of being in which mutuality is the model. Jesus commended this approach and said of top-down kinds of power, "It is not so among you" (Mark 10:43). If the first shall be last and the last first, then the realm of God will turn hierarchies of prestige and privilege upside down. We need to use power *with* others instead of *over* others.

If the ministry of all the people or, as it is sometimes called, the "priesthood of all believers," is ever to become a reality, that ministry must start somewhere. If Christian faith is to be more than conventional morality, then someone must set the pace for others to follow. If spirituality is more than unthinking legalism filled with shoulds and oughts and no joy, then someone must demonstrate the possibility of a joyful faith actually lived out.

When pastors can begin to be straightforward about our own faith journeys, other people can recognize similar movements of the Spirit in their lives. The deeper we go in our own experiences, the more general those experiences turn out to be; the more we dare to lift up the struggles and successes of our own faith pilgrimage and share them with others, the more others are helped to articulate events along the way of their own journeys. All too often laity keep their deepest religious experiences from pastors. Parishioners fear that pastors will not understand or accept their experiences. They may worry that they are not good enough. They don't show themselves for fear of rejection. They hide behind walls and hope that someone will notice them and pay attention. They hope that the pastor will say words that validate their experience.

The most significant experiences of people, the deepest moments of their lives, are those moments when God seems most real. These experiences of God both frighten and compel. They affirm that we actually can experience God's mystery in this life, a mystery that comforts and assures. At the same time, these experiences of God are awesome and numinous. Often people do not know what to make of their experiences of God. They may make either too much or too little of them.

Consider the terrible things some people believe God has asked them to do. Without help in discernment, they jump to the wrong conclusion, sometimes to their own destruction or to the detriment of those who love them most. People abandon commitments, walk out on families, harm other people, become arrogant and unforgiving because they really believe that God has called them to a particular way of life or mission.

People need help to sort out their deepest experiences. They need someone they trust to help them recognize the dangers of some choices. They need help to recognize their own tendency to spiritual pride. They need guidance to distinguish the voice of God from the welter of other voices. At heart, therefore, the pastor must be a guide to the spiritual life, a person others trust to share the struggle. The pastor offers assistance, not as one who has already arrived but as one who is on the same journey, going alongside the people and perhaps a step or two ahead.

In pastoral ministry, realizing that one has never arrived offers essential protection from spiritual pride and arrogance. The task of the pastor as spiritual guide is to point beyond himself or herself to the One who works through the everyday events of human life—sometimes in spite of human efforts to resist—in order to claim us, direct us, and bless others through us.

Because our pastoral role involves us in the spiritual lives of others, we need a deeply held spirituality that can sustain us through the struggles of darkness, doubt, and confusion. To have this inner strength, we must personally engage in the struggle that Nouwen called "the search for God" but which may be better expressed as our "pilgrimage toward God in the company of Jesus Christ." After all, we are not so much looking for a hidden God as we are struggling to find ways to make ourselves open to an encounter with the God we already know in Jesus of Nazareth. We know that God is already present with us; we seek to be conscious of that presence in our daily life. The goal is not to find God but to find ourselves caught up in God, held in the embrace of the divine and empowered as Christ's disciples to live fully and richly.

Effective pastoral ministry requires clear priorities. If we acknowledge that the quality of our life and relationship with God is central to effective pastoral ministry, then we relinquish secondary matters to focus on the primary. Time for prayer, for the nurture of our own soul; time spent in theological reflection about the contemporary situation of our world; time spent with God's Word to get our direction straight are never luxuries to be cast off at the first demand of duty. These activities are also duty. To forsake these core activities robs us of that which is central to faithful discipleship and proper authority.

Pastors need to recognize the importance of such times, to

respect our own need for soul-nurturing times, and to claim that time as part of our ministerial work. Special time with God is at the heart of pastoral ministry. Parishioners can learn to respect this time and even help the pastor claim it.

Pastors may need to insist on quiet time. The pastor's message on the voice mail could state, "The pastor is unable to answer your message now because he/she is in prayer. Please call back at.…" This message would speak clearly about the importance of prayer in the pastor's work. As the pastor indicates the need for time alone and meets that need by taking time off to pray and be alone with God, the people of the congregation will pay attention and perhaps begin to follow suit in their own lives.

Because pastors live out their ministry in relationship with congregational members, pastoral ministry also includes the willingness to recognize and be led by the spirit of God at work in the lives of these people of faith. The pastor is never the one with all the answers. We can learn much from the lives of these congregational "saints" who model Christian faithfulness. Sometimes the Spirit may make more headway in their lives than in ours. When we are going through an acknowledged dry period, the members can serve as reminders of faith, as pointers to God. Because this mutuality is so necessary, we should lift up and treasure the witness of these faithful people. We should allow them to teach and encourage us, blessing us with their faith. Thank God, the pastor does not have to do be in ministry all alone!

Authority is not necessarily a matter of the pastor against those served. Authority can be exercised jointly to the advantage of both pastor and people. Christ empowers his people, authorizing them to be bearers of the good news.

A spirit of renewal is present in the church today. That renewal is not always visible, but it is operating quietly and slowly as leaven in the loaf. The Spirit is at work, calling people to a faith far deeper than mere assent to propositions. Real faith finds its basis in an intimate relationship with God.

Pastoral ministry cannot escape the consequences of that renewal movement. Ministers can have no authority in the church of tomorrow if we try to hold on to an authority of role or office. The only authority pastors can claim is that of personal integrity. Faith communities expect this kind of authentic authority in their pastors, and they deserve to find it. Pastoral leadership is a sharing of life's deepest experiences, not by those who have all the answers but by those who feel free to examine the journey.

Epilogue

enri J. M. Nouwen ends his splendid book *Creative Ministry*
with this summary:

> Ministry calls for men and women who do not shy away
> from careful preparation, solid formation, and qualified
> training but, at the same time are free enough to break
> through the restrictive boundaries of disciplines and spe-
> cialties in the conviction that the Spirit moves beyond pro-
> fessional expertise.[1]

What Nouwen sought was a renewal of ministry that would
revitalize the Christian church in America. From the vantage
point of more than twenty-five years, we recognize Nouwen's
prophetic gift. He appreciated the need for pastoral ministry's
liberation from authoritarian institutional maintenance goals
and from reliance upon alien methodologies so a recovery of
its center may take place. This recovery must begin with a
model for ministry that does not retreat from academic work,
solid theology, and faithful scholarship with the biblical text

but is not captive to these either. Above all, renewal will involve paying attention to the movement of the Holy Spirit and being faithful to the calling to break out of our seminary restrictions. Many of us, for example, received careful training on not referring to ourselves and keeping our sermons free of all personal illustrations. We may need to break that rule in order to begin to share our journey with the people.

Most importantly, pastoral ministry needs to be a way of exercising spiritual guidance for individuals and the community of faith itself. Offered with clarity, honesty, and love, such guidance can help pull the church out of its slow decline into irrelevance. Ministers who dare to exercise our office as servants of Christ, rather than as slaves to convention or to the whim of powerful people, discover a renewed authority, which is given by Christ. Christ has called some Christians into the particular work of pastoral ministry, and Christ promises to accompany those he has called. As Christ accompanies his servants, he also empowers them for the work he sets before them. Too often we get caught up in ruts of our own making, trying to live up to the expectations of other people rather than trying to take seriously the call of Christ to us personally. Our high calling is our empowerment to break restrictive boundaries set by what we have been taught by even the best of teachers. We need to be free to follow the leading of the Holy Spirit into the unknown future. May that divine power free us from our various forms of slavery and set us on the road to a form of pastoral ministry that is rooted and grounded in Christ's powerful love.

Notes

CHAPTER ONE
A Calling Seeking Definition

1. H. Richard Niebuhr, *The Purpose of the Church and Its Ministry*, 76–77.

2. Henri J. M. Nouwen, *Creative Ministry*, xx.

3. Nouwen, 111.

CHAPTER THREE
Spiritual Direction as a Metaphor for Ministry

1. Margaret Guenther, *Holy Listening*, 27.

2. Guenther, 43.

CHAPTER FOUR
The Care of Souls as Spiritual Guidance

1. John Wesley, "Selected Writings" from *John and Charles Wesley: Selected Prayers, Hymns, Journal Notes, Sermons, Letters and Treatises*, ed. Frank Whaling (New York: Paulist Press, 1981), 165.

2. Flora Slosson Wuellner, *Feed My Shepherds: Spiritual Healing and Renewal for Those in Christian Leadership* (Nashville, Tenn: Upper Room Books, 1998), 89–90.

CHAPTER FIVE
Worship as Spiritual Guidance

1. Don E. Saliers, *Worship and Spirituality*, 31.

2. John E. Burkhart, *Worship*, 30.

3. Burkhart, 31.

4. Macrina Weidekehr, *A Tree Full of Angels*, 23.

5. Craig Douglas Erickson, *Participating in Worship*, 48–49.

CHAPTER SIX
Teaching as Spiritual Guidance

1. James D. Smart, *The Teaching Ministry of the Church*, 84–85.

2. Smart, 86.

3. Nouwen, 3–4.

4. Nouwen, 13.

5. Lewis Joseph Sherrill, *The Gift of Power*, 82.

CHAPTER SEVEN
Social Change as Spiritual Guidance

1. Nouwen, 84.

2. John R. Fry, *A Hard Look at Adult Christian Education*, 65.

CHAPTER EIGHT
Management as Spiritual Guidance

1. Charles E. Hambrick-Stowe, *The Practice of Piety*, 138.

2. John Wesley, *The Works of John Wesley*, Vol. 9, 70.

3. Howard Thurman, *With Head and Heart*, 20.

4. Tilden H. Edwards, *Spiritual Friend,* 178.

5. Charles M. Olsen, *Transforming Church Boards into Communities of Spiritual Leaders*, 39.

6. Olsen, 8.

CHAPTER NINE
The Pastor as Person: Keeping Our Souls Alive

1. G. Lloyd Rediger, "Clergy Killers," *The Clergy Journal*, August 1993, 7.

EPILOGUE

1. Nouwen, 115–16.

The Spirituality of Ministry
Bibliography

Ackerman, John. *Spiritual Awakening: A Guide to Spiritual Life in Congregations.* Washington, D. C.: The Alban Institute, 1994.

Baxter, Richard. *The Reformed Pastor,* ed. James M. Houston. Portland, Oreg.: Multnomah Press, 1982.

Barry, William A. and William J. Connolly. *The Practice of Spiritual Direction.* New York: Seabury Press, 1982.

Borchert, Gerald L., and Andrew D. Lester, eds. *Spiritual Dimensions of Pastoral Care.* Philadelphia: The Westminster Press, 1986.

Bouttier, Michel. *Prayers for My Village.* Translated by Lamar Williamson. Nashville, Tenn.: Upper Room Books, 1994.

Burkhart, John E. *Worship.* Philadelphia: The Westminster Press, 1982.

Clinebell, Howard. *Growth Counseling for Marriage Enrichment.* Philadelphia: Fortress Press, 1975.

De Koning, Neil. *Guiding the Faith Journey: A Map for Spiritual Leaders.* Grand Rapids: CRC Publications, 1996.

Dunnam, Maxie. *Alive in Christ: The Dynamic Process of Spiritual Formation.* Nashville: Abingdon Press, 1982.

Edwards, Tilden H. *Spiritual Friend: Reclaiming the Gift of Spiritual Direction.* New York: Paulist Press, 1980.

Erickson, Craig Douglas. *Participating in Worship: History, Theory, and Practice.* Louisville.: Westminster John Knox, 1989.

Farnham, Suzanne G., Joseph P. Gill, R. Taylor McLean, and Susan

M. Ward. *Listening Hearts: Discerning Call in Community.* rev. Harrisburg, Penn.: Morehouse Publishing, 1991.

Fenhagen, James C. *More than Wanderers: Spiritual Disciplines for Christian Ministry.* New York: Seabury Press, 1981.

Fiand, Barbara. *Releasement: Spirituality for Ministry.* New York: Crossroad, 1987.

Fry, John R. *A Hard Look at Adult Christian Education.* Philadelphia: The Westminster Press, 1961.

Guenther, Margaret. *Holy Listening: The Art of Spiritual Direction.* Cambridge, Mass.: Cowley Publications, 1992.

Hambrick-Stowe, Charles E. *The Practice of Piety: Puritan Devotional Disciplines in Seventeenth Century New England.* Chapel Hill, N.C.: The University of North Carolina Press, 1982.

Hands, Donald R., and Wayne L. Fehr. *Spiritual Wholeness for Clergy: A New Psychology of Intimacy with God, Self and Others.* Washington D.C.: The Alban Institute, 1993.

Holifield, E. Brook. *A History of Pastoral Care in America.* Nashville: Abingdon Press, 1983.

Hollyday, Joyce. *Then Shall Your Light Rise: Spiritual Formation and Social Witness.* Nashville: Upper Room Books, 1997.

Holmes, Urban T. *Spirituality for Ministry.* San Francisco: Harper and Row, 1985.

Job, Rueben P. *Spiritual Life in the Congregation: A Guide for Retreats.* Nashville: Upper Room Books, 1997.

Job, Rueben P., and Norman Shawchuck. *A Guide to Prayer for Ministers and Other Servants.* Nashville: Upper Room Books, 1990.

———. *A Guide to Prayer for All God's People.* Nashville: Upper Room Books, 1992.

Johnson, Ben Campbell. *Calming the Restless Spirit: A Journey toward God.* Nashville: Upper Room Books, 1997.

———. *Pastoral Spirituality: A Focus for Ministry.* Philadelphia: The Westminster Press, 1988.

———. *To Will God's Will: Beginning the Journey.* Philadelphia: The Westminster Press, 1987.

Jones, Timothy. *Finding a Spiritual Friend: How Friends and Mentors Can Make Your Faith Grow.* Nashville: Upper Room Books, 1998.

Kelsey, Morton T. *Companions on the Inner Way: The Art of Spiritual Guidance.* New York: Crossroad, 1983.

———. *Encounter with God.* Minneapolis,: Bethany Fellowship Press, 1972.

———. *The Other Side of Silence: Meditations for the Twenty-First Century.* New York: Paulist Press, 1997.

———. *Transcend: A Guide to the Spiritual Quest.* New York: Crossroad, 1981.

Killinger, John. *Bread for the Wilderness, Wine for the Journey.* Waco: Word Books, 1976.

Leech, Kenneth. *Soul Friend.* San Francisco: Harper and Row, 1977.

May, Gerald. *Care of Mind–Care of Spirit: A Psychiatrist Explores Spiritual Direction.* San Francisco: Harper and Row, 1992.

Mead, Loren B. *The Once and Future Church: Reinventing the Congregation for a New Mission Frontier.* Washington D. C.: The Alban Institute, 1991.

McNeill, John T. *A History of the Cure of Souls.* New York: Harper and Brothers, 1951.

Miller, Wendy. *Invitation to Presence: A Guide to Spiritual Disciplines.* Nashville: Upper Room Books, 1995.

Moreman, William. *Developing Spiritually and Professionally.* New York: Fortress Press, 1985.

Morgan, Richard L. *Remembering Your Story: A Guide to Spiritual Autobiography.* Nashville: Upper Room Books, 1996.

Morris, Danny E., and Charles M. Olsen. *Discerning God's Will Together: A Spiritual Practice for the Church*. Nashville: Upper Room Books, 1997.

Mulholland, M. Robert, Jr. *Shaped by the Word: The Power of Scripture in Spiritual Formation*. Nashville: Upper Room Books, 1985.

Niebuhr, H. Richard. *The Purpose of the Church and Its Ministry*. New York: Harper and Row, 1956.

Nouwen, Henri J. M. *Creative Ministry*. Garden City, N. Y.: Doubleday and Company, 1971.

———. *In the Name of Jesus*. New York: Crossroad, 1991.

———.*The Wounded Healer: Ministry in Contemporary Society*. Garden City, N.Y.: Doubleday and Company, 1972.

Noyce, Gaylord. *Church Meetings That Work*. Washington, D.C.: The Alban Institute, 1994.

Olsen, Charles M. *Transforming Church Boards into Communities of Spiritual Leaders*. Washington D.C.: The Alban Institute, 1995.

Peacock, Larry. *Heart and Soul: A Guide for Spiritual Formation in the Local Church*. Nashville, Tenn.: Upper Room Books, 1992.

Peterson, Eugene H. *The Contemplative Pastor: Returning to the Art of Spiritual Direction*. Grand Rapids: Wm. B. Eerdmans, 1989.

———. *Under the Unpredictable Plant: An Exploration into Vocational Holiness*. Grand Rapids: Wm. B. Eerdmans, 1994.

———. *Working the Angles: The Shape of Pastoral Integrity*. Grand Rapids: Wm. B. Eerdmans, 1987.

Rediger, G. Lloyd. *Clergy Killers: Guidance for Pastors and Congregations under Attack*. Louisville: Westminster John Knox, 1997.

Rice, Howard L., and Lamar Williamson Jr. *A Book of Reformed Prayers*. Louisville: Westminster John Knox, 1998.

Rice, Howard L. *Reformed Spirituality: An Introduction for Believers*. Louisville: Westminster John Knox, 1991.

Rutter, Thad. *Where the Heart Longs to Go: A New Image for Pastoral Ministry.* Nashville: Upper Room Books, 1997.

Saliers, Don E. *Worship and Spirituality.* Philadelphia: The Westminster Press, 1984.

Sherrill, Lewis Joseph. *The Gift of Power.* New York: The Macmillan Company, 1955.

Smart, James D. *The Teaching Ministry of the Church: An Examination of the Basic Principles of Christian Education.* Philadelphia: The Westminster Press, 1954.

Steere, Douglas V. *Dimensions of Prayer: Cultivating a Relationship with God.* Nashville: Upper Room Books, 1997.

Thayer, Nelson S. *Spirituality and Pastoral Care.* Philadelphia: Fortress Press, 1985.

Thurman, Howard. *With Head and Heart: The Story of Howard Thurman.* New York: Harcourt Brace Jovanovich, 1979.

Vest, Norvene. *Gathered in the Word: Praying the Scripture in Small Groups.* Nashville: Upper Room Books, 1996.

Wesley, John. *The Works of John Wesley.* Edited by Rupert E. Davies. Nashville: Abingdon Press, vol. 9, 1988.

Whaling, Frank, ed. *John and Charles Wesley: Selected Prayers, Hymns, Journal Notes, Sermons, Letters and Treatises.* New York: Paulist Press, 1981.

Wiederkehr, Macrina. *A Tree Full of Angels: Seeing the Holy in the Ordinary.* San Francisco: HarperSanFrancisco, 1988.

Wuellner, Flora Slosson. *Feed My Shepherds: Spiritual Healing and Renewal for Those in Christian Leadership.* Nashville: Upper Room Books, 1998.

———. *Release: Healing from Wounds of Family, Church, and Community.* Nashville: Upper Room Books, 1996.

The Group Lectio Process

Prepare.
Take a moment to come fully into the present. Sit comfortably alert, close eyes, and center yourself with breathing.

1. Hear the word (that is addressed to you).
First reading (twice). Listen for the word or phrase from the passage that attracts you. Repeat it over softly to yourself during a one-minute silence. When the leader gives the signal, say aloud only that word or phrase (without elaboration).

2. Ask, "How is my life touched?"
Second-stage reading. Listen to discover how this passage touches your life today. Consider possibilities or receive a sensory impression during the two minutes of silence. When the leader gives the signal, speak a sentence or two perhaps beginning with the words *I hear, I see, I sense*. (Or you may pass.)

3. Ask, "Is there an invitation here?" (for you).
Third-stage reading. Listen to discover a possible invitation relevant to the next few days. Ponder it during several minutes of silence. When the leader gives the signal, speak of your sense of invitation. (Or you may pass.)

4. Pray (for one another's empowerment to respond).
Pray, aloud or silently, for God to help the person on your right respond to the invitation received.

If desired, group members may share their feelings about the process after completing these steps.

Group Lectio on Life Process

THE GROUP LECTIO ON LIFE PROCESS includes these steps, slightly elaborated to assist the leader in practice.

Prepare.

1. Hear the word.

Review recent life events and select a single incident for reflection.

• Give several minutes of silence for reviewing the hours and experiences of the last several days. Allow one event or situation to keep returning for attention.

• Ask group members to state simply the approximate time of day when their chosen incident occurred.

2. How is my life touched?

Review the incident mentally and emotionally as it happened, then be receptive to a phrase or image that seems to be given in relation to it:

• Remind the group that "touched" refers to the touch of Christ.

• Ask them to recreate the incident as it actually happened, remembering all they can about sights, sounds, etc.

203

Allow one to two minutes for this undertaking.
• Ask them to recreate the emotions of the incident:
Where was the strongest energy or any major energy shift?
Allow one to two minutes for this.
• Ask them to set aside mentally all their musings after
two or more minutes, and let their minds become receptive to a phrase or image from scripture or literature.
• Remind them after two minutes to be aware that the
given phrase or image is a blessing, a sign of Christ's presence in the incident. Ask group members to share only the
phrase or image.*

3. **Is there an invitation here?**
Offer the incident and your reflections back to God. Rest
and be responsive to any invitation that might come.
• Ask group members to bring back to memory their
life incident and their image or phrase alongside it. Allow
one minute to hold both in peace.
• Urge them to offer up everything to God mentally, to
let it go for now.
• Ask them to be receptive to any invitation or encouragement that may come now to be or to do something in
the next few days. Allow about one or two minutes of
silence.
• Ask the members to share their invitation.*

4. **Pray for the person to the right.**
Afterward, the group members may share their thoughts
and feelings about the process, if desired.

*Note: Anyone may pass at any time.

About the
Author

HOWARD RICE is a native of Wisconsin and a lifelong Presbyterian. He graduated from Carroll College in Waukesha, Wisconsin, and from McCormick Theological Seminary in Chicago. He became pastor of the House of Faith Presbyterian
Church in Minneapolis and later was instrumental in organizing a merger of three small struggling congregations to develop
a new church in an inner-city, west side Chicago community.
The call to San Francisco Theological Seminary in 1968 as
Professor of Ministry involved him in student placement for
internships and vocational counseling. He retired from this
position in 1997.

Howard has been married to Nancy Lee Zoerb Rice for
over forty years. They are the parents of two daughters: the
Reverend Wendy Rice Dreitcer and Amanda Marie Hernandez. They have four grandchildren: Hannah and Monica
Dreitcer and Ezra and Amala Hernandez. Howard is an ama-
teur oil painter and a lover of music. He sings in his church
choir and collects recordings of twentieth-century classical
music.